The Golden Laws

The Golden Laws

HISTORY THROUGH THE EYES OF THE ETERNAL BUDDHA

Ryuho Okawa

Lantern Books • New York
A Division of Booklight Inc.

Lantern Books
A Division of Booklight Inc.
One Union Square West, Suite 2001
New York, NY 10003

Library of Congress Cataloging-in-Publication Data

Okawa, Ryuho, 1956-
[Ougon no ho. English]
The golden laws: history through the eyes of the eternal buddha/
Ryuho Okawa; [translated by The Institute for Research in Human
Happiness, Ltd.].
p.cm.
Rev. ed. of: The laws of gold. c1990.
ISBN 1-930051-61-1 (pbk.: alk. paper)
1. Kofuku-no-Kagaku (Organization) 2. Spiritual life. I. Okawa,
Ryuho, 1956-Laws of gold. II. Kofuko-no-Kagaku (Organization) III.
Title.

BP605.K55 033 2001
299'.93—dc21
2001045967

Table of Contents

Chapter Three: Eternal Mountains and Rivers

Chapter Four: The Land of the Rising Sun

Preface to the First Edition

It is my pleasure to issue *The Golden Laws*, the second in the trilogy on the topic of the Truth, following on from the publication of the first, *The Laws of the Sun*. While the latter discusses "enlightenment of the whole" as well as the "enlightenment of individuals," thus clarifying the whole picture of the Truth, this book deals principally with theories of time and history.

The first chapter presents methods for changing your life into gold and living a truthful life. It also explains right self-realization based on the Truth. The next three chapters discuss the work of Guiding Spirits of Light who have appeared in the West, the East, and specifically Japan. Chapter Five covers the history of the most important prophets, such as Zeus of ancient Greece and Jesus Christ. The last chapter outlines, century by century, forthcoming events, from the twenty-first through to the twenty-ninth century and beyond, focusing on the unfolding of the Truth in the future.

In this book I have attempted to publicize a true history of how Buddha's plan has unfolded on Earth with the passage of time. Once we know the truth of history, we cannot help but become aware of the historical significance of our mission in the present age.

The objective of *The Golden Laws* is basically in accordance with the ideas of the German philosopher Hegel, who wrote *Philosophy of History* as "the development and realization of World Spirit." The present volume is both a book of historical philosophy and a philosophical book on the Truth. In that it outlines five thousand years of human history as seen from the Real World, it is a book that has never before been written, and perhaps never will be written in the future. Receiving inspiration from my subliminal consciousness, which is existent in the ninth dimension in the heavenly world, I think I have made this difficult subject matter comprehensible even to young readers.

I sincerely hope that you will enjoy reading this treatise on history and that it will stimulate your mind.

Ryuho Okawa
June 1987, for the first Japanese edition

Preface to the Revised Edition

Numerous arrows of Light have already been released. *The Golden Laws* is the embodiment of a new golden arrow that represents El Cantare's view of the history of the world. At the same time, it presents a bird's-eye view of the spread of the Universal Truth as it flows according to El Cantare's plan.

The work of the high spirits known as Bodhisattvas[1] and Tathagatas[2] of Light described in this book reveal the secret history of humankind and the values of Lord El Cantare, the supreme being of the terrestrial spirit group, otherwise known as the Buddha. His wish is to establish the universal Truth. In this book, a clear distinction is made between the values of Heaven and Hell. This book also thoroughly explains the transmission of heavenly values to the West, the East and Japan through different genealogies of Light.

"The time has come for the scions of Light, who have been scattered throughout the world, to awaken. The age in

---

1. Bodhisattva : see p. 11.
2. Tathagata : see p. 9.

which the Truth will be preached on a global scale has finally arrived. You must work to build utopia on Earth, overcoming differences of nationality by acting simply as inhabitants of this planet. In the past you were all children of Buddha working together to spread the Light, and you shall remain so both now and in the future. Cast aside all hatred and embrace love. Do not mourn over differences but rejoice in the equality of your Buddha-nature. The new millennium will be full of hope." This is the message that El Cantare offers.

Ryuho Okawa
July 1995, for the revised Japanese edition

Chapter One
Creating a Golden Life

1. Magic to Make Each Day a Golden Day

To some people, the time allotted to them in this world seems very long whereas, to others, it is not nearly long enough. Whatever its content, however, a life can be divided into the equivalent of morning, noon and night. You cannot reverse the direction of these divisions any more than the sun can go backward. You are always in the present. The past only provides material for contemplation now, and the future is unknown. Each and every person, without exception, is living the single day of "now."

Life is a succession of such nows, and if we want to live a fulfilled life, we must strive to make each and every day worthwhile. If you wish to live a golden life, you have to turn each day of your life into a golden day. Once you have succeeded in turning each day of your life into gold, your whole life will emanate a golden light.

Victory or defeat in transforming your life into a golden one depends on how you use every twenty-four hours. How efficiently you can use the total of the time available to you will determine your success or failure. No matter how rich or poor you may be, how powerful or ordinary, you are all equal in the face of time. The day consists of only twenty-four hours.

Although it is possible for us to borrow money, we cannot borrow time. Although we can save money, we cannot save time, or gain interest on it that could result in a twenty-five hour day. The time we did not use yesterday cannot be carried over and used today, any more than we can borrow tomorrow's time for use today.

I have started writing this book but I cannot use time from yesterday to complete the job, any more than I can use time from tomorrow. The only time I have is today's twenty-four hours. For this reason, I am writing it one letter at a time and whether or not these letters turn into gold and find their way into the hearts of my readers depends on how I use each second of each of the twenty-four hours. The magic to turn each day into gold, for me, too, depends on how I utilize each and every second. While nobody goes through their life with a stopwatch in hand, counting each second as it passes, the time appropriated to each life is steadily slipping away like sand in an hourglass, whether people are conscious of it or not.

A child, born naked into this world, can create a unique life for itself, depending on how it decides to use time. It could be said that the magic that changes our lives into shining golden ones is at the same time the secret of converting time into the quality of life.

2. The Truth of Time

Everything you can think of, good and evil, beauty and ugliness, truth and untruth is all contained within the flow of time. Like the stars in the Milky Way, the individual's life, and in fact the total history of humankind, are contained within the currents of time.

If you could pick up the flow of time and study it, I am sure that you would be surprised. The flow of time is like a long, thin tube stuffed with everything imaginable and calling out to be seen. I am not speaking metaphorically, as you will see when you return to the Real World where the Akashic Records are kept. If you are capable of reading these, you will find that they contain the complete history of humankind and nearly everybody who sees them is astonished to learn the secret history of the human race. However, only the inhabitants of the eighth or ninth dimensions in the Real World are able to read the Akashic Records. The reason for this is that a complete knowledge of human history provides an understanding of Buddha's plan and His blueprint for future society. This is something that may not be shown to just anyone.

Among those in recent history who have seen the Akashic Records in the Real World while still incarnate on Earth, we find Emanuel Swedenborg (1688–1772), a northern European mystic, and the Austrian philosopher

Rudolf Steiner (1861–1925) who founded the Anthropos-
ophy movement in the early twentieth century. The souls of
both these people were inhabitants of the Tathagata Realm
of the eighth dimension. Further back in history, at the time
of Jesus, we find St. John who performed astral travel to see
the Akashic Records and then recorded what he had learned
in the "Book of Revelations." St. John, too, was an inhabitant of the eighth dimension.

However, the Akashic Records are not written down in
book form and different people interpret them in different
ways. To those who are permitted to see them, the records
appear as a three-dimensional motion picture that is played
before their eyes, but people's interpretation of what they
see depends on their personal degree of enlightenment. It
usually appears in a symbolic form that has to be deciphered
by the viewer. The apocalyptic vision of the future of
humankind that John presents in the Bible was only a single
symbolic view and cannot be described as a full vision.

At present, Elijah, St. John, and Nostradamus[1] are
among those in the eighth dimension who have been given
the task of safeguarding the Akashic Records, while
Gautama Siddhartha (Shakyamuni Buddha) and Jesus

---

1. Michael Nostradamus, or Michel de Nostredame, (1503–1566) was a
   French physician and astrologer who treated many victims of the bubonic
   plague epidemic in Europe. He is probably best known for his mysterious
   book on predictions of the future, called *The Centuries*. However, his style
   of predictions was written in extremely symbolic and ambiguous quatrains,
   which can be interpreted in a variety of ways.

Christ in the Cosmic Realm of the ninth dimension hold the key to them.

Time is not something that can be measured by a clock of this world alone. Time is like the music that can be heard when the Akashic Records are looked at in the Real World. To make this a little easier to understand, think of a record that has two hours of classical music engraved on its surface. In its own way it represents two hours of time that have been confined within an inanimate object. Now, if there was someone who could see the music that exists within the grooves of the disc, it would mean that they could enjoy the whole two hours of music in the space of a moment. However, ordinary people are not capable of this feat and we have to put the record on a turntable and listen to it for the full two hours. Herein lies the key to understanding the secret of time and the history of humankind. To put it simply, past history represents those records that have already been played, while future history is those that have yet to be placed on the turntable. Ordinary people are incapable of understanding the music contained within the records until they have heard it played, but those with the ability to see the tune engraved on the surface of the records are capable of acquiring a remarkably clear understanding of the future.

The Akashic Records are not confined to the general history of humankind, they also contain records of each individual soul. These are known as the individual "thought tape," and can be used by high-ranking spirits to reveal the three lives of a living individual, that is to say, their past, present and future. This is the Truth about time.

3. The Secret of the Thought Tape

I would like to explain what is meant by the "thought tape." In his teachings, Shakyamuni Buddha spoke in great detail on the law of karma. Jesus also referred to this law when he said, "as man sows, so shall he reap." More simply, the law of karma has been explained as the law of action and reaction.

Now let me explain the relationship between these teachings and the thought tape. People have known about the law of cause and effect since ancient times, saying that good deeds will be rewarded while God will punish those who commit evil deeds. Some suppose that this was taught to people for ethical reasons, simply as a way of creating a society that is comfortable to live in. However, this was not the case. The human "mind" is not merely a moralistic existence, but was created according to the Physics of the Light of Buddha. This rule states that the universe exists according to Buddha's will, and that the cosmic laws are governed by the Physics of the Light of Buddha. In other words, the laws that control this world and those realms beyond can all be attributed to the various qualities of the Light of Buddha. This is an idea that is supported by the majority of physicists in the Real World.

The Physics of the Light of Buddha are based on three clear theses. The first states that the Light of Buddha is amplified when it comes into contact with something with which it finds an affinity, whereas it avoids contact with all objects that are opposed to it. This is what Jesus Christ meant when he said, "For unto everyone that hath shall be given, and he shall have abundance: but from him that hath not shall be taken away even that which he hath" (Matthew 25:29). In other words, those who have an affinity with the Light of Buddha will be blessed with ever more Light, whereas those whose characters reject the Light will become increasingly deprived of it. This is the truth. It has been said that, "If the clouds are cleared from your mind it will be filled with the Light of Buddha whereas if they remain, they will cut off the Light of Buddha and be the cause of suffering in your life." Shakyamuni Buddha taught that the root of all suffering lay in an attachment to physical desire and that until these attachments have been removed the Light of Buddha would not shine, and true happiness could not be achieved.

The Ten Commandments, which Moses brought down from the mountain, illustrate that, by discarding evil and choosing good, we create an affinity with the Light of God. Confucius preached that the way to greatness was the way to serve heaven and the road to happiness. It can be seen from this that all the great men of history understood and taught the first thesis of the Physics of the Light of Buddha concerning the affinity and rejection of the Light of Buddha.

The second thesis states that creation and destruction occur through the process of condensation or diffusion of the Light of Buddha. For instance, if the Light of Buddha is condensed through willpower for a particular purpose, a spiritual entity may appear. If these vibrations are further condensed, it can result in the appearance of a material object. The opposite is also true; if the objective consciousness of the will is relaxed, a material object can lose its form. A spiritual entity will have to change its shape in order to exist when the Light of Buddha starts to be diffused. Consequently, the process of creation of the human spirit and the human body can be understood through the condensation and diffusion of Light.

The third thesis states that the Light of Buddha has wavelengths—higher frequencies are attuned to other high frequencies and the lower frequencies are attuned to other low frequencies. The Light of Buddha contains thought waves that are imbued with the will to communicate, which are transmitted throughout the Grand Cosmos, including multi-dimensional space. However, these thought waves are only capable of communicating with others of the same frequency. For this reason, people living on Earth cannot communicate with spirits of the higher realms unless their consciousness is on an equal level. People who find it easy to communicate with the spirits on the lower planes do so because their consciousness is in tune with that of the lower spirits.

If a member of a certain religious group insists that there are tens of people in their order who can communicate with the Tathagata Realm of the eighth dimension and hundreds in contact with the Bodhisattva Realm of the seventh dimension, it is untrue. Only people with a spiritual consciousness equal to that of the inhabitants of the Tathagata Realm can communicate with the eighth dimension while living on Earth.

Let us look now at the people in Japanese history who have been able to accomplish this. Apart from Ame-no-Minakanushi-no-Kami (God Ruling the Center of Heaven; see Ch. 4:1) and Yamato-Takeru-no-Mikoto (see Ch.4:3) of Japanese mythology, there has only been Prince Shotoku (574–622; see Ch.4:4), the Buddhist monk Kukai (774–835; see Ch.4:6) and, more recently, the philosopher Kitaro Nishida[2] (1870–1945; see Ch.2:2). As you can see, it is a very small number. Shinran[3] (1173–1262; see Ch.4:8) and Dogen[4] (1200–1253; see Ch.4:9) are from the Bodhisattva Realm, and as for the founders of the so-called "new religions," hardly any of them can hope to be described as Tathagata.[5] Even those who are serious men of religion belong to the Light Realm of the sixth dimension at

---

2. Kitaro Nishida (1870–1945): a philosopher of the Kyoto school, originally from Ishikawa Prefecture, Japan. He taught at Kyoto University.
3. Shinran (1173–1262): a Japanese Buddhist monk. Founder of *Jōdo Shin-shū* (True Pure Land School of Buddhism).
4. Dogen (1200–1253): a Japanese Buddhist monk. Founder of *Sōtō-shū* (Sōtō School of Buddhism).
5. Tathagata is a word originated from Sanskrit that describes a Great Guiding Spirit of Light who resides in the eighth dimension in the Real World. A Tathagata is an embodiment of Absolute Truth, a being who manifests love toward humans and instructs us. The Japanese word for Tathagata is Nyorai. Refer to *The Laws of Eternity* by Ryuho Okawa (Lantern Books, 2001), Chapter 5: The World of the Eighth Dimension.

best, whereas eighty or ninety percent of them are merely puppets of the devil in hell.

Now that I have explained the three theses of the Physics of the Light of Buddha, we have to understand that a human being's true form is a "light body," and that we carry within us the qualities of the Light of Buddha.

In accordance with the first thesis, if your mind retains an affinity with the Light of Buddha through love, goodness, beauty and truth, you will live a happy life. If, on the other hand, you harbor hate, anger, jealousy, suspicion, complaints and selfishness in your mind, these feelings will repel the Light of Buddha and lead to a life of misery.

According to the second thesis, if you hold positive thoughts, you will remain both spiritually and physically healthy. Alternatively, if you tend to think negatively, sickly thoughts are created that will eventually manifest themselves as an illness of the body. Cancer, in particular, is a phenomenon of unhealthy thoughts, and so if you let your mind take in the Light of Buddha, and you hold positive thoughts, the cancer is certain to disappear.

The third thesis tells us that if we strive to change our mindset so it becomes in tune with the higher spirits, it will bring us happiness, but if we attune ourselves to the lower spirits, we will become progressively discontented.

The human mind was created through the concentration of Buddha's Light under a clear intention. One part of it, called the "thought tape," acts as a kind of recording tape and is invested with the magnetic energy of Buddha's Light.

This tape contains a record of everything that person has thought and done from the past down to the present day. The record of the thoughts and deeds that have an affinity with the Light of Buddha are as if written in gold, while those that reject the Light of Buddha are gray. For this reason, it is possible to tell at a glance what kind of a person somebody is by looking to see if their thought tape is shining gold or clouded gray.

The law of karma means that the course of your life is dictated by the color contained within your thought tape. Those who have a lot of gold in their thought tape will live a golden life, that is to say the life of a Bodhisattva[6] of Light. At the other extreme, those with a large quantity of gray in their thought tape will live a gray life, which means that an ordeal awaits them in hell.

However, there is a mysterious secret to the thought tape; even though your thought tape may be written with letters of gray, if you are truly repentant for your thoughts and deeds, they will change to gold. The truth is that if you mend your ways, your life will shine with a golden light.

4. A Future That Shines with a Golden Light

The thought tape contains a record of all your lives, from the ancient past down to the present day, and also incorpo-

---

6. Bodhisattva is a word originated from Sanskrit that describes an Angel of Light who resides in the seventh dimension of the Real World. A Bodhisattva dedicates him- or herself to enlightening and saving people thorough the will of Buddha. The Japanese word for Bodhisattva is Bosatsu. Refer to *The Laws of Eternity*, Chapter 4: The World of the Seventh Dimension.

rates the law of karma. In the same way that a musical tune does not suddenly break down in disharmony, the melody of our lives also has a steady rhythm and tone, so that no matter what part of the thought tape you look at, it will not be radically different from the rest of it. Therefore, if you fill your heart and mind with love and compassion in accordance with the Truth, it will show in your actions, and the record will surely be written in letters of gold. However, if you speak negatively or think and do things that result in the unhappiness of others, it will all be written in gray letters. If you allow your temper to get the better of you, your anger will be written in letters that are blood red. If you become obsessed with sex and become a slave of disharmonious acts with members of the opposite sex, it will be recorded in pink letters. If you are quick to find fault with others and spend your time searching for defects in their character, your thoughts will be noted in green letters, the color of reptilian eyes. Cowardice, meanness, unease, and worry about the past and future are written up in indigo letters. People who cling to sickly thoughts, who are always complaining to others of their illnesses, have this written in letters the color of dried mud.

These colors—the red, pink, green, dark blue and brown—combine to produce an indescribably unpleasant shade of gray. Therefore, for a person with a gray tape like this to change it into shining gold, he or she has to undergo an inner revolution of Copernican scale. Without this radical change in perspective of life, it is impossible to grasp a golden future.

It goes without saying that in order to allow your future to shine like gold, it is necessary to fill your thought tape with golden script. In other words, your thoughts and deeds must shine with a golden light. However, even if your tape already contains letters written in gray, these can be converted to gold through right self-reflection. If you live in accordance with right prayer, your future, too, will start to sparkle with a golden light.

5. True Self-Realization

When considering a future that shines with a golden light, our thoughts naturally turn to self-realization. The term self-realization has become very popular these days, particularly in the West, where methods to attain success through self-realization are widely discussed. This concept is spreading widely in Japan, too.

When looked at from the standpoint of Truth, there are two sides to the theory of self-realization and success. Let us first look at one of the correct sides. The basic idea behind self-realization is that if you think about a desire in concrete, tangible, visible terms and concentrate on it every day, it will eventually be attained in a way that you had never even imagined. This is quite true, and in the Real World self-realization through willpower and prayer is an everyday occurrence. Therefore it can be said that this aspect of self-realization is just an example of applying the rules of the Real World to the world on Earth in order to achieve success and wish fulfillment.

However, although the theory is correct in itself, the problem is whether or not the people who use it are pure in heart. This is a very important question. You must never forget that misguided self-realization is the same in effect as reserving a seat on the express down to hell. In other words, you must be careful not to aim for the wrong destination. You must determine whether your self-realization will lead you toward Buddha, or heaven, or if it will take you in the direction of the devil, that is to say, down to hell. This is a question you must ask yourself all the time. You can determine whether or not an aim of self-realization is correct by asking the following questions:

1. If your ambition were realized, would it lead to the happiness of the people around you, to the happiness of all the people in the world?
2. If you succeeded in realizing your ambition, are you sure that it would not cause unhappiness to others?
3. If your ambition were to be achieved, would it improve you as a person?

If you can answer "yes" to all three questions you will know that your goal is a true one and your prayer is right.

There are sure to be some spirits in the Real World, from the fourth dimension and above who will respond to a strong desire or prayer, regardless of its content. However, if you do not think of others and pray merely for reasons of egoistic self-interest, your thoughts will eventually communicate themselves to the inhabitants of hell. As a result, although your plans may seem to go well for a while, you will eventually be possessed by the spirits of hell and fall completely under their control. This will lead inevitably to sickness, failure in business, or despair.

Many people pray for recovery from illness, but this too has its dangers. Unless you apologize to Buddha for your past mistakes, fully repent of your sins, and show true gratitude to the people around you for everything they have done for you, you will arrive at the mistaken idea that you will find happiness as long as your physical body is healed.

This will put you deeper in the clutches of the spirits of hell and your illness will become progressively worse. This kind of problem is much more common than you may think.

The same is true of those people who think that all they want in life is to become rich and famous. What will you do if you become wealthy? What will it mean if you become famous? You should ask yourself these questions. If you want to become famous in order to be able to do something for the people of the world, then it is a good desire. However, if you just want to sit in a big chair and boast of your achievements, then it is wrong. If you only wish to make money in order to lead a life of luxury, be careful, this desire is a danger signal. Of course, if you want to control large sums of money to use for right purposes, then obviously it is a good goal.

Success and wealth are not evil in their own right, but they both lie in the heart of Buddha. Therefore, if you wish to attain certain goals in your life, it is essential that you do so with a correct perspective of life and right understanding of your mission and purpose. When good people become very successful and develop as human beings, it represents a ray of hope for the world.

Here, I feel that I must warn you to make sure that you understand the intention that lies behind your desire. There is no need for me to tell you what will happen if you direct your thoughts toward hell; but what will happen if all you can think of is obtaining supernatural power or being able to perform miracles that are impossible for anyone else to achieve? Thoughts of this kind are attracted to the realms where *Tengu* (long-nosed spirits living in mountains that possess spiritual powers) or *Sennin* (hermit wizards) inhabit and, eventually, you will be influenced by them. You will become increasingly eccentric and people will treat you as if you were mad.

When I talk of the supernatural, I mean things like bending spoons, levitation, fortune-telling and commercial hypnotism. When you try to perform these kinds of skills, remember it may be with the help of the *Tengu* and *Sennin* Realms, or it might even be the devil himself who is helping you to achieve them. The high spirits of the Major Heaven would never concern themselves with this kind of thing.

However, if you live a life filled with a love for your fellow humankind, the self-realization you pray for will be true self-realization, the high spirits will hear you and a world of peace and harmony will unfold for you.

6. The Bridge of Love

I have talked at length about self-realization, but the true reason we are born into this world is to undergo spiritual discipline, to refine and improve our present state, and to strive to advance ourselves. If this is included in our idea of self-realization, daily improvement is daily success. However, there is also a danger. When seeking self-realization, we tend to seek profit and happiness for ourselves alone and not give enough thought to others. The harder you wish for self-realization, the more you must concentrate on the importance of love. Then the greater the degree of self-realization, the greater the amount of love you must hold.

As you draw nearer to realizing your goal, you must take the time to check the degree to which your love has developed. In order to achieve this, you should always bear in mind what I wrote in *The Laws of the Sun* about the developmental stages of love—love has four stages that are known as "love for loving (fundamental love)," "spiritually nurturing love," "forgiving love" and "existence as love." As you gradually advance from one stage to the next, your love becomes ever deeper and larger. These stages also represent the stepping stones to human perfection and the way to self-realization.

No matter how engrossed a person may become in obtaining wealth, position and fame in this world, it will mean nothing after he has died and returned to the Real World. He may be prime minister of the country or the president of a major business, but once he dies and falls to hell, he will not find anyone there who is impressed by the title on his business card. If he is lucky enough to return to the heavenly realm, he will find that there is no opportunity for him to use his business card any longer. The only thing that holds any meaning in heaven is the purity of his heart, the level of his enlightenment and the record of his life that is written on his thought tape. If a man becomes a billionaire in this world and is able to enjoy every luxury, this will not serve as a passport for him to enter heaven. He may own a yacht and a private jet but he can no more take them with him than he can his luxury home or his savings. No matter how famous he may have been on Earth, it will not impress the devils one whit or lower the temperature of the cauldron in which he stews.

The same is true of worldly honors. You may be elected to the academy or awarded a medal, but it will mean nothing. Hell is full of former ministers, university deans, professors, judges and attorneys who bemoan their fate. They feel that it is only natural for others to be punished in this way, but they cannot accept that they could have fallen so far. This is the fate that awaits those who think only of their own honor and do not offer their love to others. Even men of religion are not exempt.

Using clairvoyance, I have witnessed the agony of a religious man who once received a medal for contributing to world peace but is now suffering in hell, rolling on the ground, unable to bear the pain in his head. His teachings had been mistaken, and the greater esteem in which his memory is held by his followers on Earth, the worse his suffering becomes. I have also seen a man who was an influential spiritual leader when he was alive, claiming that everybody could perform miracles like those of Jesus Christ, but now he is screaming and suffering in the flames of hell. While it is true that he deserves some praise for providing many people with spiritual awareness, he should have realized that without the help of the high spirits of heaven we cannot receive the light of heaven to purify the possessing spirits of hell. In order to receive this guidance, we must purify our minds to put them on the same wavelength. There is a basic flaw in the teaching that all men can perform miracles like those of Jesus Christ. People who are possessed cannot provide others with Light and this is the point he had failed to understand. Self-realization for those who aim to become religious leaders is also extremely difficult. You should be particularly wary of religions that promise divine favor in this world on Earth.

First you must learn to love yourself as a spiritual existence, but you must not stop there. If you love yourself, try giving love to others. Love was given to us by Buddha.

That is why you must not monopolize it for yourself, but share it with others. In this way, love will link you with others, creating a "Bridge of Love."

7. The Miracle of Life

Are human beings creatures who should be happy to live in mediocrity, to run hither and thither aimlessly like ants? Of course not. If the Buddha you believe in is the Buddha of love, the Buddha of compassion, then surely he will have provided you with the chance to become more than a mere ant. He offers the chance of rebirth and the opportunity to remove the scales from your eyes.

The moment the scales are removed from your eyes, what does it mean? It is the moment in your life when a miracle occurs. If you become short-sighted, you look for some glasses, you go from shop to shop looking for the glasses or contact lenses that satisfy you. So why is it that you do nothing when you cannot see other people's hearts, when you cannot understand the object of life, when you can no longer see the other world, when you do not understand the will of Buddha? How can you remain calm when you cannot see the Truth? You must realize that several layers of scales have formed over your eyes and that your real eyes will be unable to see until these have been removed. You cannot see the reality of the world, nor will you be able to detect the workings of the high spirits either. So what kind of people suffer from these scales over their eyes? I would like now to offer some examples. First there are doctors. Their job is to dedicate themselves to the study of human life and they often deal with patients who are hovering between life and death. However, if we look at modern-day medical practitioners, we see that they do not understand the true meaning of death, and are even incapable of determining the moment when death occurs. They talk of brain death and say that death occurs the moment that the brain ceases to function, but this is wrong.

Death occurs in humans when the soul leaves the body and the silver cord that binds the two is broken. It is only once this has occurred that a person can truly be declared dead, and at no other time. The soul usually leaves the body anywhere from several hours to one day after the heart has stopped. This means that even after all the bodily functions appear to have ceased, the spiritual body still fills the physical body, and the spiritual heart continues to beat. Not realizing this, doctors remove organs or parts of the eyes from dying people as soon as the brain waves terminate, but they have no way of knowing the shock and confusion their ignorant actions create in the dying person. The fear their actions cause not only hinders the person on their departure to the next world, but also complicates the job of the guardian spirits who have come to lead them away. Organ transplants that are carried out without spiritual knowledge do not represent an advance in medicine. They are merely a denial of the dignity of the human soul in the name of materialistic medical science. Doctors need to study more about the soul; they need to realize the truth that, at the time of death, our souls are the same shape as our bodies, with a heart, a stomach, and hands and feet that function exactly the same as their physical counterparts.

Another example of people who are blinded by the scales that cover their eyes is that of some Buddhist priests. There are priests who neither believe in nor understand the world after death but who nevertheless chant sutras and perform services merely for financial gain. It is quite outrageous, but a large number of them fit into this category. The priests' real work is to guide those souls who have only recently found themselves in the spirit world and are still suffering from confusion. This is the true meaning of the services that are held for the deceased.

The dead will not be saved by a ritual reading of the sutras. First, the priest needs to understand completely the contents of the scriptures and convey them as a concept to the dead through will. Then the bereaved need to be taught the purpose and mission of human beings on Earth so they will see for themselves that their grief is uncalled for. That is the true mission of all priests, not to take advantage of the relatives of the deceased and charge huge sums for posthumous Buddhist names as if these were some kind of merchandise.[7] This kind of attitude is inexcusable. Not a single soul in the other world answers to its posthumous name; no matter how much the name may cost, it will not

---

7. Offering of the posthumous Buddhist name to the deceased is a common custom in Japan. In practice, the bereaved family members ask a Buddhist priest to create a name for the deceased that will be engraved on the tombstone or memorial tablet to be enshrined in the family altar.

lighten the burden of the souls suffering in hell in the slightest.

In order to be saved from the torment of hell, it is necessary for each person to recognize the error of their ways, to repent them and to pray to Buddha for forgiveness. In other words, the responsibility for a person falling into hell lies with the individual, not with their family. The bereaved should try to continue to live bright, happy lives as this will allow the soul of the deceased to rest easy and become aware of the mistakes it committed during life. This is far more important than continuing to grieve over the deceased. The bereaved should also continue their religious studies, then the resulting power of virtue and the light of enlightenment will ease the soul of their loved one. They should pay tribute to their lost ancestors with the light of Truth and demonstrate through their lives how the children of Buddha should act.

Doctors and priests are not the only people whose sight is obscured by the scales of ignorance; such people are legion and another good example is judges. Laws do not judge people. Laws that people have created through consensus are not capable of judging the past of a human soul. The experts may argue about niceties such as whether the basic law above the positive laws should be called "Nomos" or "Nomoi," but we must never forget that all law originates from the Truth. The rule of law means the rule of Buddha's Law and therefore judges must strive to understand the will of Buddha before they pass judgment on others.

There was a professor of law who once tried to apply a system of quantitative analysis to crimes in order to systematize the process of law, but this was a total mistake. In my spiritual travels, I once saw a supreme court judge who was suffering in hell from a guilty conscience. In life he had not believed in spirits and had scoffed at the idea of life after death, so he had never hesitated to hand down the death penalty. However, after he died, he realized his mistake and his conscience allowed him no peace. Be they judges, prosecutors or attorneys, all specialists at law should study the Truth before even considering judging another human being. All law springs from the Truth and claiming ignorance of this is no excuse. In other words, they must remove the scales from their eyes before proceeding with their chosen profession. This is essential, and once they have achieved it, a miracle is sure to occur in their lives.

8. The Right View of Work

The vast majority of humans dedicate the greater part of their lives to a particular line of work. The German word for an occupation is "Beruf," which means literally "God's calling." This is because we learn God's will and find ways of achieving it through our work.

People who are always calling out to God are not necessarily admitted to heaven any more than those who recite the name of the Buddha are guaranteed a place in paradise.

Most people tend not to be involved with religion so deeply. The only contact they have may be when they visit a church, shrine or temple, or attend a funeral, a memorial service or wedding. However, I do not intend to criticize them for their lack of faith. Rather than dedicate themselves to some false religion and destroy the happiness of their homes, lose their money, their health and dignity, it is much better for them to dedicate themselves to their career and live a good and prudent life.

It is a fact that there are numerous scientists, businessmen and artists who belong to the higher realms of the spirit world without even suspecting the existence of such a world. For instance, Albert Einstein lives in the Tathagata Realm of the eighth dimension where he still continues with his studies into physics. The Japanese physicist, Hideki Yukawa[8] (1907–1981) is active in the Bodhisattva Realm of the seventh dimension together with the mathematician, Kiyoshi Oka[9] (1901–1978) whose present subject for study is *The Beauty of Mathematics and the Beauty of Enlightenment.*

The thinker Philip Gilbert Hamerton (1866–1946), author of *The Intellectual Life*, is living in the Bodhisattva Realm of the seventh dimension, as is the science fiction

---

8. Hideki Yukawa (1907–1981): a Japanese physicist who was born in Tokyo and graduated from Kyoto University. He proposed a new field theory of nuclear forces and predicted the existence of the meson. He was awarded the Nobel Prize for Physics in 1949 for research in the theory of elementary particles.

9. Koyoshi Oka (1901–1978): a Japanese mathematician who was born in Wakayama Prefecture and graduated from Kyoto University. He devoted himself to the study of the theory of functions of several complex variables.

writer H. G. Wells, who is still actively studying future science. The great Japanese author Soseki Natsume (1867–1916) has returned to the Bodhisattva Realm where he too remains involved in his writing. Recently he published a work in the seventh dimension entitled *A Life of Love and Beauty*, which was very well received.

Among the businessmen now living in the Bodhisattva Realm we find the car manufacturer Henry Ford, the steel magnate Andrew Carnegie, and the financial tycoon John D. Rockefeller. They are now working on the theme of modern society and management. Among the artists, Picasso is now active in the Brahma Realm, the highest part of the Bodhisattva Realm. In the field of music, Johann Sebastian Bach lives in the Tathagata Realm of the eighth dimension where he is composing heavenly music. Mozart lives in the Bodhisattva Realm where he is working on Christian music. Beethoven lives in the lower area of the Bodhisattva Realm. He now aims to transcend the sadness evident in parts of his music and become an expert in the music of joy.

While I am on the subject, other well-known composers are situated as follows: Handel—Tathagata Realm; Wagner—Bodhisattva Realm; Schubert—Light Realm (sixth dimension); Chopin—Brahma Realm; Vivaldi—Bodhisattva Realm; Tchaikovsky—Light Realm; Mahler—Tathagata Realm; Brahms—Light Realm; Bruckner—Light Realm.

Music fans might be interested in listening to how the level of enlightenment of each composer is manifested in his music. Stanislav Bunin—a genius of the piano who was born in the Soviet Union, defected to the West and is now active in Japan and other Western countries—is in fact a highly advanced spirit of the Bodhisattva Realm and his guiding spirit is Chopin. Heaven planned the spread of Truth in the materialistic states of the Soviet Union through the arts.

As you can imagine, not all high spirits involve themselves in religious work. Many of them are engaged in a variety of professions as they discipline themselves in this Earthly world. Therefore, if we manage to get to the top of our chosen occupation, and work for the sake of the people of the world, we will be working in accordance with Buddha's will and practicing His Truth. This means that even people who do not believe in the Real World and who get the shivers at the very mention of the word "religion" might still be living according to the Truth.

9. To the Glorious Goal

Now, it can be said that you are getting closer to the glorious goal of creating a golden life. A golden life is one that dazzles the eye with its golden splendor; it is light itself.

Before we are born, each of us belonged to a different realm, in a different dimension of the spirit world. Then our spirits lodged themselves in our mother's womb, and when we were born to this world, we were all equal. In other words, we all started from the same starting point. Through His mercy, Buddha causes us to lose all the memories of our previous lives in order that we may all dedicate ourselves equally to our soul training.

For instance, if a child was born who could remember having been Michelangelo or Leonardo da Vinci in a previous existence, do you think this would help him to live a happy life? Even if the child was destined to become an artist in this life, the memory of his previous life would not necessarily help him. It would be much better if he were to begin by scribbling pictures of cows and horses like the other children. There is plenty of time for him to realize his potential as he grows older and this would allow him much more scope to improve his soul.

There was no need for Jesus Christ to have been born of the Virgin Mary. He could have been born like any other child; there was no necessity for him to be singled out as the Savior in that way. In the same way, it was not necessary for Shakyamuni Buddha to be born from the armpit of Queen Maya. Even though he was destined to save humankind, he could have been born as an ordinary child, played and studied with other children and, as he matured, to have begun to question the meaning of life. Later, he could have started his religious studies in earnest, realizing the true way to live, before eventually attaining enlightenment and saving the peoples of the world. In this way he would become a true savior.

A true leader should begin from the same starting line as anyone else, then gradually move forward to lead the race. If the leader starts a hundred meters in front of the starting line and calls back for everyone to follow him, the others will lose the desire to compete. Effort is essential when aiming to reach the glorious goal. It is impossible for anybody to become great without effort. No matter how great a person may become eventually, they all have the same beginnings. A person's greatness is measured by his broad-mindedness and the loftiness of his aspirations. In order to achieve this we need to go through various experiences in life. Your objective on this Earth should be to become as close as possible to Buddha. There is no other true goal in life.

The image of a person who is close to Buddha varies according to our environment, education, ideas, beliefs, customs, abilities and talents. In the same way that seven colors of light emanate from Buddha, so does the image of being close to Him vary from person to person. Therefore, we must all think deeply about how we should live, what we should do to become accomplished human beings and in so doing become closer to Buddha. This is something that each of us must consider most carefully.

People who think that life is limited to their time on Earth and that everything ends at death will be constrained by their own thinking. However, those who believe that the essence of a human being is an immortal soul and an eternal life will realize that life is merely a stage through which they pass to grow closer to Buddha. It is not a choice of whether you believe or not; it is a fact that the Real World exists and humans are all eternal travelers, but some choose to aim for the glorious goal, whereas others fall by the wayside like a worn-out shoe.

10. Immortality and Eternity

I would like now to look once more at the question of desire, that is to say, why it is that we humans find ourselves at the mercy of our desires. Lust is driven by an instinctive desire to preserve the species. Without realizing it, humans are preoccupied by the wish to continue the thread of life. Next we have the craving for rank and fame. This springs from the desire to have our names recognized by the greatest number of people in order that, even after we have died, we will not be forgotten. The hunger for money reflects a desire to express our existence through material goods, becoming intoxicated through worldly gain. People with such a desire find daily confirmation of their lives in shining pearls, sparkling jewels, huge houses or deluxe cars. They become intoxicated with the feeling of indestructibility these possessions provide.

Putting it simply, a longing for immortality lies behind all humankind's desires. The truth is that if it were possible, we would probably like to live a healthy life until we were two hundred, five hundred, even a thousand years old. However, as we know that this is impossible, we look for some other way by which to achieve immortality. In other words, our fear of death manifests itself in desire.

This craving for immortality exists within groups as well as individuals. Office workers are often so eager to see their company last forever that they devote themselves to their job, like the samurai in ancient times who served their lords devotedly, holding the prosperity of the lords' lineage as the supreme command. However, despite all their efforts, it is practically impossible to foresee a company that will last even one hundred years.

Also, some people are willing to throw their lives away in wars for the sake of an intangible concept known as the "state." It does not seem to worry them that the state would cease to exist if all its people died; instead they are quite happy to devote their lives to furthering its existence. In this way, people look for immortality through economic units known as private companies or political units known as states, but why should this be? It is because we all must die.

We are all equal before death; no matter who we are, we are all equal in the solemn fact that we are destined to die. Kings, nobles, beauties and philosophers, none of them will be able to escape death. That is why humans search so desperately for "immortality" through rank, fame or wealth. However, it is all an illusion; it is like believing that we will live forever through having our name engraved on a stone monument.

Realizing that personal immortality is unachievable, some people try to identify themselves with economic or political activity. They like to think that even though they may die, their company or political party will continue to grow. Unfortunately, however, twenty years after the retirement of the most powerful company president, there is usually nobody in the company who can even remember his name. In this way, his dreams of immortality will come to nothing in the end.

The Roman Empire was once thought to be invincible but it disappeared after a few hundred years—where are the souls of the soldiers who shed their blood to protect it? In the end, it is plain that it is impossible for humankind to obtain immortality in this world either individually or through a financial or national unit.

However, there is another state that, although essentially different to immortality, could be described as being its twin, and this is "eternity." Although humankind is denied immortality in this world, it can still hope for eternity. So what is this "eternity"? It is manifested in human beings who live within the Truth. Nothing in this world lasts forever, but by living within the Truth, we exist within eternity, we live in an eternal present. Living in the Truth means to understand that we are the children of Buddha and as such we can live forever through reincarnation. The fact is that our souls are only incarnated in this world temporarily in order to allow us to improve our state.

When we live in this Truth, we are free of the curse of death and can fly through eternal time and infinite space. We should not think of ourselves as mortal, as valueless objects to be cast off like rags; the pitiful pile of bones crouching inside a grave is not our final state. After death, we are once more free to continue our existence, and this is why you should discard your dream of immortality and enter the way to eternity. There you will find the great river of true life.

Chapter Two
Rushing Across the Earth

1. The Spell of Materialism

In this chapter I would like to take a closer look at the Truth from an ideological point of view. In his book, *The Open Society and Its Enemies* (1945), the philosopher Sir Karl Raimund Popper (1902–1994) refers repeatedly to "the spell of Plato," and I would like to explain what he meant by this.

Popper believes that the primary task of philosophers should be to release humankind from the ignorant taboos and simple animism of primitive society and lead it into the bright new world of rationalism. Despite this, however, he claims that the Greek philosopher Plato preached soul worship and the kind of simple reincarnation of the soul that was believed in by primitive peoples, thereby forcing the people out of the sunlight and back into the caves. Popper states that a society that believes in proof, logic, and science is an "open society," whereas one that believes in souls and the afterlife holds its people spellbound and forces them into obscurantism, thus creating a "closed society."

While I admire Popper for the time and effort he obviously put into his magnum opus, to be quite frank I have to say that the basic concept behind it is mistaken. For all his talk of rationality, it was Popper who was trying to imprison people in a "closed society." Plato had actually striven to lead the people into an "open society."

Plato was a Great Guiding Spirit of Light from the Tathagata Realm of the eighth dimension who was incarnated in Greece. Like his mentor, Socrates, he experienced astral travel while living in this world and made numerous trips to the heavenly realm. He taught that the Real World of truth, goodness and beauty—the world of the Idea—existed behind the phenomenal world. This Ideal world is in fact the home of the high spirits. To use the Buddhist terms for the realms he described, they were the Diamond Realm and the Matrix-store Realm.

Popper based his philosophy on his own knowledge and experience of this Earthly world whereas Plato's philosophy was based on his experience not only of this, the three-dimensional world, but also of the fourth dimension and beyond. Any intelligent reader should be able to tell which of the two men was in a position to talk about "open" and "closed" societies. A philosophy that claims that humans exist only in this world belongs to a "closed society," whereas a philosophy that states that humans live in both this world and the other world represents that of an "open society."

It is quite clear that Plato knew about the Real World. In his book, *Phaedo* he introduces Socrates and has him give a clear description of the Real World and the way in which the soul undergoes reincarnation. Both Plato and Socrates produced intellectual explanations of the Truth, foreseeing the rise of a Western civilization that would be based on the intellect.

There are numerous anecdotes told of Socrates. One time, he is said to have stood motionless for a day and a night. There has been a lot of speculation among modern philosophers as to what he was meditating on, but the answer is quite simple. Socrates' soul had left his body and was busy conversing with the high spirits in the upper dimensions. His wife, Xanthippe, is described as being the epitome of a bad wife, but in reality she was just a practical woman and unable to understand her husband's eccentricities.

2. The Essence of Greek Philosophy

Socrates lived in the fifth century B.C., which is approximately the same period that Shakyamuni was active in India and Confucius preached in China. At the beginning of a new age, Buddha always sends a number of high spirits to Earth to perform His work simultaneously in this way. The same phenomenon can be witnessed at the end of an era, too. If we have an overview of history, we realize that groups of extremely highly developed people appear in a particular area at a particular period. For instance, this can be seen thirty-seven to thirty-eight hundred years ago in Greece when Zeus was alive, twenty-four to twenty-five hundred years ago when Socrates was active, and also in Rome during the days of the empire. The same phenomenon can be observed in Britain in the seventeenth and eighteenth centuries and in America during the nineteenth and twentieth centuries.

In Japan, a large number of Tathagata and Bodhisattva appeared twenty-seven to twenty-eight hundred years ago when, led by Amaterasu-O-Mikami (the Sun Goddess), they created a theocracy that was to become the foundation of the nation state of Yamato.[1] The members of the present imperial family are direct physical descendants of these figures.

To return to Greece, it first began to prosper in approximately the eighth century B.C. with the rise of the autonomous city-state known as the "polis." The sixth century B.C. saw the appearance of a statesman called Solon who, in order to help impoverished farmers and bring peace between the aristocracy and commoners, cancelled all debts, banned debt-slavery, and extended political rights. Solon was in fact a Tathagata who was later reincarnated in Japan during the sixth century when he was known as

---

1. Old name for the country around Nara Prefecture in Japan today.

Shotoku Taishi (or Prince Shotoku). His brother soul[2] was incarnated in America in the nineteenth century as Abraham Lincoln and was responsible for the emancipation of the slaves.

Athenian culture reached its peak in the time of Pericles (495–429 B.C.) and democracy thrived. Pericles was also from the Tathagata Realm and a branch of his spirit was reincarnated in Japan in the eighteenth century as Sadanobu Matsudaira (1758–1829), who successfully carried out a series of political and social reforms.

At around the same time, Socrates (469–399 B.C.) appeared and began to teach about the existence of objective truth as well as the integration of knowledge and virtue, explaining the essence of intelligence through dialogue. As I mentioned earlier, his disciple Plato (427–347 B.C.) systematized the idealistic philosophy that stated that Idea is the only true existence. Despairing of the existing society within the city-states, Plato wrote of an ideal political structure that would be led by a philosopher-king.

Plato's ideal of a state existing under a philosopher-king has been compared to the communist nations and their

---

2. The soul that resides in the human body is only one part of the spiritual whole; in the subconscious level, the soul is connected to its own bigger entity that remains in the Real World. The spiritual body consists of one core spirit and five branch spirits, and they are called brother or sister souls. Each of the six comes down to Earth in turn to carry out their spiritual refinement. For example, Prince Shotoku and Abraham Lincoln are two brother souls which reincarnated in turn from the same spiritual body group. Refer to *The Laws of the Sun* by Ryuho Okawa (Lantern Books, 2001), Chapter 2: The Truth Speaks.

dictatorial leaders of the twentieth century. However, this is a rather superficial view. The materialistic viewpoint of the present day stands in direct opposition to Plato's spiritual philosophy. Rather than being looked at as the forerunner of communism, Plato's denial of private ownership of property or the communal ownership of women should be considered to be more of a denial of the ego and personal avarice from a religious perspective. In fact, it is similar to the idea of egolessness and renunciation of the world as practiced in Buddhism.

Plato was reincarnated in Germany during the eighteenth century as G.W.F. Hegel (1770–1831), who completed the idealistic philosophy initiated by Immanuel Kant (1724–1804) and developed the Hegelian Dialectic, which is a concept of formation and development. Hegel published numerous works, the most famous being *The Phenomenology of Mind*, *Science of Logic*, and *Philosophy of Right*. In his life as Hegel, his philosophy was closer to that of Aristotle. He sought to explain the Truth rationally and intellectually in a form that would appeal to contemporary society, and, for this reason, he was unable to experience astral travel as he had done as Plato. However, as can be seen in his *Philosophy of History*, he had a clear idea of God's plan for the world and was receiving guidance from Socrates in heaven.

Later in Greece, we see the appearance of Aristotle (384–322 B.C.). Aristotle criticized the idealism of his teacher, Plato, and preached substantialism, whose central idea was a scientific method to capture universal reality through concrete facts, thus laying the foundation for many branches of learning. He was also a member of the Tathagata Realm and the main characteristic of his teaching was an emphasis on logic, a tendency that is readily seen in such works as *Metaphysics*, *Nichomachean Ethics*, and *Politics*. Aristotle was later reincarnated in China during the Sung dynasty as the Zen priest Hui-kai, who wrote *The Gateless Barrier*, a commentary on forty-eight Zen koans in which he tried to explain the state of nothingness. In this way, the father of European philosophy led a revival of Oriental philosophy.

After his incarnation as Hui-kai, Aristotle was reborn once again as Kitaro Nishida (1870–1945), a famous Japanese philosopher of the Kyoto school. Nishida's central thesis, influenced by his previous incarnation, leaned toward the Japanese philosophy of nothingness; but his original plan was to resolve contrasting philosophies of the East and West into a higher unity. In other words, he planned to build a philosophy on the "synthesis" of thesis-antithesis-synthesis.

It can be seen from all this that as well as standing in the mainstream of Western studies, Greek philosophy also found its way into Oriental thinking, and I think that this demonstrates the magnificent scale of Buddha's plan. The essence of Greek philosophy is none other than the Truth.

3. Eternal Rome

The polis society of ancient Greece eventually collapsed, and Rome moved to the forefront of culture. In the beginning of the third century B.C. (295 B.C.), Rome unified what is now known as Italy. Then in the year 30 B.C. Alexandria fell, and Julius Caesar's nephew Octavian, who controlled the entire Mediterranean world, became the first Emperor, Augustus. For the following two hundred years people were able to live in peace under what came to be known as Pax Romana. During this period Rome inherited the culture of Greece while being influenced by Christianity, which began in Judea with the teachings of Jesus Christ (4 B.C.–29 A.D.).

The period up until the fall of Rome to Germanic tribes in 476 A.D. is known in Western history as the Ancient Classical Period. Then, the period up until the fall of Constantinople, that is to say of the Eastern Roman Empire, in 1453 A.D. is known as the Medieval Period, while the period after that is called the Modern Age. I would like now to give you an outline of the history of the Truth up until the fall of the Western Roman Empire or what was known as "Eternal Rome."

Cicero (106–43 B.C.) was a philosopher who was born in this region and is representative of the end of the republican period. Like Plato, Cicero wrote several treatises, among which were *On the Laws*, *On the State*, and *On Duties*. He was strongly influenced by Greek Stoicism, particularly by Zeno (336–263 B.C.), criticizing positive law and defending natural law, while emphasizing the importance of equality. Cicero was an inhabitant of the Brahma Realm that lies between the Bodhisattva Realm of the seventh dimension and the Tathagata Realm of the eighth dimension. He was later reincarnated in China as Chu Hsi (1130–1200) who was a thinker of the Southern Sung dynasty and who compiled the teachings of Confucius, founding the Chu Hsi school of Confucian thought.

Another Stoic philosopher was Seneca the Younger (4 B.C.–65 A.D.), who is famous for *The Brevity of Life*, an analysis of frivolous pastimes. Although he appeared rather pessimistic in his writings, Seneca was an inhabitant of the upper area of the Bodhisattva Realm. He was later to be reincarnated in Germany as Arthur Schopenhauer (1788–1860), who developed a unique form of pessimistic philosophy.

Yet another philosopher of the Stoic school was Emperor Marcus Aurelius (121–180 A.D.) who is famous for his work, *Meditations*. He was reincarnated in Geneva in the eighteenth century as Jean-Jacques Rousseau (1712–1778), who was very active in France during the Enlightenment. Rousseau is most famous for his works, *Discourse on the Origin of Inequality among Men*, *Confessions*, and *Emile*. He was an idealist and believed strongly in the dignity of human beings. Marcus Aurelius who was later to become Rousseau was a high spirit from the upper areas of the Bodhisattva Realm.

Next came Plotinus (204–270) who, although he was originally born in Egypt, became one of the most famous philosophers of the Roman Empire. He established a new interpretation of Plato's philosophy, known as Neoplatonism. While strongly influenced by Plato, Plotinus took a mystical rather than rationalist position. Whereas Plato took a dualistic view of the phenomenal world and the world of Idea, Plotinus emphasized oneness, saying that oneness existed before human subjectivity and objectivity were separated, and claimed that this was the True Existence or God. He also claimed that the three-dimensional world emanated from ultimate reality and this is known as the emanation theory.

Plotinus was later reincarnated in Japan as Masaharu Taniguchi (1893–1985), who founded the religious group named Seicho-no-Ie (House of Growth) and preached a philosophy that illuminated the Truth of life. Although Taniguchi was Plotinus in his previous incarnation, before that, in around 760 B.C., he had been born in Kyushu, the southern main island of Japan, where he was known as Izanagi-no-Mikoto (see Ch.4:2). In this form, he is known as the physical father of the Sun Goddess, Amaterasu-O-Mikami (see Ch.4:2), when she was incarnated in this world. This spirit, who was incarnated in turn as Izanagi-no-Mikoto, Plotinus, and Taniguchi, now lives in the Brahma Realm.

Toward the end of the Roman era a great Christian thinker, St. Augustine (354–430), appeared. He is most famous for his huge work, *The City of God*. In his younger days, Augustine was fascinated by the dualism of good and evil, Manichaeism, as preached by the Persian religious leader, Mani (215–275). Later, being influenced by his master, St. Ambrose, Augustine learned about Plotinus' philosophy and developed the idea that a Christian "City of God" would appear through the struggle with the "City of Earth." He was later reborn in Germany in the nineteenth century as the philosopher Martin Heidegger (1889–1976), best known for his work, *Being and Time*. He was originally from the Tathagata Realm.

4. Utopian Thought in the Middle Ages

The Middle Ages drew gradually toward their close and with them the set patterns of medieval thought. With the dawn of modern times, a marked trend toward utopian thought became apparent and I would now like to look deeper into this philosophy.

The Middle Ages are generally considered to have ended in 1453 when Constantinople fell to the Muslims and the Byzantium Empire was destroyed. Already almost one thousand years had passed since the fall of the Western Roman Empire. By the middle of the fifteenth century, the universality of the renaissance world and the unity of the Church were beginning to fade and sovereign states were being formed. At around this time several utopian philoso-phies grew up.

The idea of utopia is not a new one. It can be seen in the paradise that Christians believe will last for a thousand years after the final Judgment Day. This belief itself was inherited from the Jews before them. To go back further in history, Plato's ideal political state, united under the rule of philosopher-kings, can also be described as a utopian dream.

St. Augustine's "City of God," which was mentioned in the previous section, refers to a heaven on Earth or the emergence of a utopian land of the Eternal Buddha in this world, and to this extent it is the same as the other theories. Although the contents may vary somewhat from person to person, the essential message remains the same. It refers to the efforts of the high spirits to create the heavenly kingdom of light that exists in the Bodhisattva and Tathagata Realms of the Real World, here on Earth.

The first to coin the word "utopia" was Thomas More (1478–1535), who lived under the absolute monarchy of the Tudors during the first period of land enclosures. In his book *Utopia*, More presents an imaginary island and describes the ideal society that exists there. On this island, there is no private property; it is an egalitarian, communal society in which the majority of the inhabitants are involved in agriculture or manual work within a planned economy. Unlike Plato, More does not think of sharing the women; rather, he puts the emphasis on a family system, based on equality. In *Utopia*, More stressed education and advocated a new cultured class of people, numbering under five hundred, who would be responsible for handling the political roles. In other words, by producing outstanding people through education, the political system would become self-reproductive and able to weather the passing of time. More's utopia practiced religious tolerance, but atheists were not given protection by the law, worship of God being an essential requirement.

Thomas More lived in Greece in an earlier incarnation as Xenophon (430–354 B.C.), one of the disciples of Socrates, and who is famous for having written *Memoirs of Socrates*. Like Plato, Xenophon was also from the Tathagata Realm in the eighth dimension.

The next person to produce a blueprint for utopia was the Italian Tommaso Campanella (1568–1639). Campanella spent twenty-seven years in prison, and this experience caused him to develop understandable if not suitable anti-establishment tendencies and his philosophy acquired a strong sense of victimization. Three years after being imprisoned, he produced *The City of the Sun*, a book in which he described an ideal state based on a Christian theocracy. His view of the perfect world was one in which all economic life is planned and the country is ruled by three governors who represent power, knowledge, and love. His plans to increase production through astrology and witchcraft remain medieval in concept, but he foresaw a time when people would only have to work four hours per day (More foretold a six-hour working day) due to advances in science and technology. On this point, it could be said that he predicted a society that will in all probability come into being in the twenty-first century onward.

It would appear that Campanella experienced visions of St. Augustine several times while he was in prison and it was from him that he learned how God's world was organized. In his previous incarnation, Campanella had been born in ninth century B.C. Sparta as Lycurgus, a famous jurist who had laid the foundation of future Spartan prosperity. Campanella had been very knowledgeable about politics, as can be seen from his book *Monarchs of Spain*, and this can be said to be due to the fact that he retained certain memories from his previous existence. At present he is an inhabitant of the Brahma Realm.

A third utopian philosopher was Francis Bacon (1561–1626), a renowned politician and the founder of British empiricist thought. He is famous for coining the phrase, "knowledge is power," which illustrates that he was at odds with the traditional medieval ideal of a life of cloistered meditation. He considered knowledge a tool that could be used to obtain power and maintained that man could use this knowledge to conquer nature through the understanding of natural laws.

Bacon published his views on utopia in a book entitled *New Atlantis* (1627). He took the legendary continent of Atlantis that was described in Plato's books *Critias* and *Timaeus* and used it to replace More's utopia, creating a New Atlantis to be situated in America. Bacon looked for the principle of happiness in science and technology, attaching great importance to the systematic development of technology. He named the royal institute in New Atlantis the "Solomon Academy."

Although it is not a widely known fact, Bacon was a psychic and could remember having lived on the continent of Atlantis ten thousand years earlier in a previous incarnation. He also had memories of having been Solomon, son of David and King of Israel (reigned c.971–c.932 B.C.). As can be seen from his *Essays*, Bacon was an extremely intelligent man, even a genius, but he was unable to forget his life as Solomon when he lived at the height of luxury and this led him to strive for political power. He reached a high post, but eventually was removed from office for accepting bribes. After returning to heaven, he spent approximately one hundred years in repentance and is now back in the Tathagata Realm.

When Immanuel Kant (1724–1804) came to the forefront of German philosophy, Bacon guided him intellectually from heaven. Looking back over these various utopian ideals, it is obvious that all of them were planned in the Real World with the aim of creating a world of the Eternal Buddha here on Earth.

5. A Storm of Religious Reformation

In addition to the utopian movement, religious reform also swept Europe from the end of the Middle Ages up until the beginning of the Modern Age. This was all part of the heavenly project to present the people with a plan for an ideal society through utopian discussion as well as to reform the unchanging monolithic structure of the Church.

Reformation was not limited solely to Europe; a similar trend could be seen in Japan starting in the Kamakura period (1192–1333), when the priest Nichiren (1222–1282) began a reformation of Buddhism based on the Lotus Sutra. He emphasized action, using the Lotus Sutra[3] as the guideline. Nichiren criticized the traditional Buddhist authorities, basing his teachings solely on religious texts, and in this he is comparable to Martin Luther (1483–1546), who appeared two hundred years later preaching theology, saying that humans are justified by their faith alone, and by so doing, summoning forth the storm of reformation.

Like Nichiren, Luther was a passionate man who would let nothing stand against him. But he was not as reckless as the Italian reformer Girolamo Savonarola (1452–1498), the "unarmed prophet," who was later taken by the people, hanged, and burned at the stake. Nonetheless, on October 31, 1517, at the age of thirty-four, Luther fastened his list, the "Ninety-five Theses," to the door of All Saints Church, Wittenberg, protesting against the selling of indulgences by the Vatican to raise money, ostensibly for the rebuilding of St. Peter's in Rome. After that, Luther began the fight in earnest. He was a nervous man and not very brave, but the words of the Roman Catholic bishops, who said that the sound of each coin falling in the collection tray took a man's

---

3. The Lotus Sutra is one of the earlier Mahayana Buddhist scriptures. It explains the teachings of the Buddha, using many allegorical stories.

soul closer to heaven, wakened his sleeping conscience and turned him into a veritable tiger.

In 1520, Luther published three treatises on religious reformation in quick succession: *To the Christian Nobility of the German Nation*, *The Babylonian Captivity of the Church*, and *The Freedom of a Christian Man*. The extent of his enthusiasm for the cause can be seen in the fact that of two hundred and eight pamphlets that were published in Germany that year, a total of one hundred and thirty-three were written by Luther. Furthermore, while he was under the protection of the elector Friedrich III of Saxony, having been declared an outlaw by the Imperial Diet of Worms, he translated the New Testament from the original Greek into German in a mere three months. Luther's teachings can be summed up as follows:

1. Priesthood for all
2. The absolute authority of the Bible
3. Religion of conscience.

However, there was a secret side to Luther that was never recorded in history. In the summer of 1517, Luther heard the voice of a spirit and later even became able to see it in corporeal form. This is the event that was to trigger his later actions. The spirit was none other than the Archangel Michael and it spoke to him saying, "You and I are one and the same. You must rise up and fight against the corruption of Rome to save the souls of the people, taking your conscience and the Bible as your weapons." Although he did not know it, Luther was actually a spirit from the Tathagata Realm of the eighth dimension and the Archangel Michael was his brother soul. Michael had once appeared in Greece where he was known as Apollo. Another part of this life form had lived on Earth as the Hebrew prophet Amos, and later in history as Martin Luther, the leader of the reformation movement in Germany.

The wave of reformation continued across Europe and the next to stand up against the Vatican was the Swiss priest, Ulrich Zwingli (1484–1531). He was a part of the life form that had previously been incarnated in Arabia, where he had been known as Mohammed (570–632) and had founded Islam. He is now living in the Tathagata Realm of the eighth dimension. The next to take up the reins of the reformation movement was the Frenchman John Calvin (1509–1564). Forced to flee from persecution in France, Calvin traveled to Basel, Switzerland, where he wrote *Institutes of the Christian Religion*, then moved to Geneva where he practiced theocracy. Whereas Luther had separated the human conscience from the power of worldly authorities, Calvin taught that this world was a place where humankind should dedicate itself to God, a place to express the glory of God and to live a life as a tool of God. After this, Calvin advocated hard work as enshrined in the Puritan ethic "worldly asceticism"—as it was called by Max Weber. It was thanks to Calvin that the rich, who had hitherto been denied access to the kingdom of God, now found themselves admitted, and the gears of modern industrialism and Christianity were finally able to mesh.

However, the fatalistic undertones of "predestination" as preached by Calvin were misunderstood by later generations. He had been trying to explain the principle of karma, but people took it to mean that humankind was divided into two groups, those whom God would save and those whom He would not. In addition to this, in order to realize a theocracy, Calvin called for the execution or banishment of over five hundred people, including the Italian humanist Baldassare Castiglione (1478–1529) and the Spanish theologian Michael Servetus (1509?–1553)—an act that resulted in general censure and confusion in the heavenly realm. Castiglione and Servetus were both high spirits and even though they may have disagreed during discussions about creed, Calvin's decision to have them banished or killed caused a great deal of distress among the inhabitants of the higher realms. Calvin had been an inhabitant of the Tathagata Realm in the eighth dimension, but now he lives in the upper area of the Light Realm in the sixth dimension where he is disciplining himself to remove his impurities. Puritanism as preached by Luther and Calvin soon crossed over to Britain where it manifested itself in a type of theocracy under the Lord Protector, Oliver Cromwell (1599–1658).

6. Modern Political Principles and the Truth

Cromwell became leader of Britain, unifying politics, the military, and religion. However, he was too eager in carrying out his puritan policies and has gone down in history as a dictator. He attempted numerous reforms including those of the judicial system, public morals, education, and religion, but his ideas were too advanced for his time and the people could not understand what he was trying to do. As a result of this, Cromwell gradually came to live the life of a recluse. Cromwell was a reincarnation of the great Athenian statesman Cleisthenes, who lived at the end of the sixth century B.C. Cleisthenes overthrew the ruling tyrant, established democracy, and prevented the reappearance of any future tyrants through the establishment of a system of ostracism. The spirit that was both Cleisthenes and Cromwell dwells in the Tathagata Realm of the eighth dimension. Having seen that theocracies like those of Calvin or Cromwell were unable to continue for long, the high spirits in the heavenly realm decided to change their policy.

What they decided was to separate modern politics from religion and take a philosophic approach toward creating a democracy. To this end, John Locke (1632–1704) was sent down to live in Britain where he founded British empiricism. His most important work on this subject, *An Essay Concerning Human Understanding* was published in 1690, the same year that he produced his main work in political theory entitled *Two Treatises on Government*. In this latter work, Locke proposed the theory of the separation of powers and stated that the legislature, based on the parliament, should have supremacy. Furthermore, he proposed that the state should be established solely on the consensus of its citizens, an idea that was the forerunner of social contract theory. John Locke, one of the great spirits of the Tathagata Realm, had in the past been incarnated as the great Athenian orator, Demosthenes (384–322 B.C.).

After Locke, another high spirit was sent down to Earth from the heavenly realm and was incarnated in France as Montesquieu (1689–1755). In 1748, he published a book entitled *The Spirit of the Laws* in which he proposed the idea of checks and balances among the threefold powers and the bicameral system of government. In this way, the Truth began to manifest itself in this world in a realistic, rational and concrete manner. Montesquieu now resides in the Brahma Realm and, during Japan's imperial restoration in the latter half of the nineteenth century, he offered guidance to major statesmen, Kaishu Katsu (1823–1899), Aritomo Yamagata (1838–1922) and other figures.

The third Guiding Spirit of Light to be sent down to Earth was incarnated as Jean-Jacques Rousseau (1712–1778) and, as explained earlier in this chapter, he was a reincarnation of the Roman Emperor, Marcus Aurelius. Having been a Stoic in his previous lifetime, Rousseau appeared this time as a philosopher of enlightenment and is famous for his books *Discourse on the Origin of Inequality among Men*, and *The Social Contract*. His most famous expression was, "All men are born equal, yet everywhere they are in chains."

7. The Appearance of German Idealism

As time passed, people found it increasingly difficult to believe in the simple worship of God or theocracies practiced by those closer to God, and began to search for a more intellectual form of "God's Law." The same was true of their understanding of God; they could no longer accept a mysterious intuitive faith or sensuous approach to God, and demanded something that could be demonstrated through intellect and reason.

As a result, a meeting was held in the Tathagata Realm of the eighth dimension, called by the spirit that had once been incarnated as Thomas Aquinas (1225–1274), one of the greatest Christian thinkers of the Middle Ages. He is famous for writing *Summa Contra Gentiles* and *Summa Theologia,* and went on to found the Scholasticism school of philosophy (which recognizes the division between faith and the unifying body of this world, while trying to reconcile the two) by effecting the philosophical synthesis of faith and reason. In his philosophy he is said to rank with Aristotle. He was a great systematizer and, acting on his suggestion, it was decided to create a philosophy of intellect and reason, based in modern Germany, that would act to spread the Truth in an academic fashion. This would encourage the spread and study of a philosophical holy law by scholars around the world in future generations.

The result of the meeting led by Aquinas was the decision to send a Great Guiding Spirit of Light to Earth in the form of Immanuel Kant (1724–1804). In a previous incarnation, Kant was born in the sixth century B.C. when he was the prophet Daniel, who appears in the book of the same name in the Old Testament. Daniel was captured by the Babylonians and interpreted the dream of King Nebuchadnezzar, prophesying the doom of Babylon and the rise of other nations.

The former prophet was reborn in modern times and this time became a great organizer of knowledge, publishing the books *Critique of Pure Reason*, *Critique of Practical Reason*, and *Critique of Judgment*. He made a thorough analysis of human existence and produced a unique outlook on the world. In addition to his *Groundwork of the Metaphysic of Morals*, he published an essay entitled *Perpetual Peace* in which he laid out the framework for the United Nations of the future. His ideas were a hundred years before their time, but this is only to be expected of a man who was a prophet in his former life. There is something in the essence of his idealistic philosophy that is common to Buddhist philosophy. Actually, many of the students of idealistic philosophy had been monks in India, Tibet or China in previous lives where they studied the Buddhist sutras. However, they are unaware of his lives as they devote themselves to their studies in their present lives.

Kant was a spirit from the Tathagata Realm, and among the other scholars of German idealistic philosophy we see Johann Fichte (1762–1814) and Friedrich Schelling (1775–1854), who were sent down from the Bodhisattva

Realm. Fichte is particular for being a behaviorist, and when it came to practical philosophy he pushed Kant's philosophy forward in a more active direction. From the winter of 1807 to early 1808, he delivered a series of lectures entitled "Addresses to the German Nation" in which he encouraged feelings of nationalism in the German people, who were still suffering from a sense of bewilderment after their crushing defeat at the hands of Napoleon. Schelling felt that greatest degree of unity between spirit and nature could be found in art. With his philosophy of identity, he laid the philosophical foundation for the Romantic movement.

Next to appear was an even greater philosopher, Georg Wilhelm Friedrich Hegel (1770–1831). As I stated earlier, he was a reincarnation of Plato, the man credited with having laid the foundation of Greek philosophy. He was one of the most intelligent people ever to have been born in this world and is one of the Christian Angels of intelligence (cherubim) who lives in the highest reaches of the Tathagata Realm in the eighth dimension, which in a narrow definition can be called the Sun Realm. Socrates and Kant live in the same environs and all of them are guided directly by Gautama Siddhartha (Shakyamuni Buddha) and Zeus, who both exist in the ninth dimension.

Hegel left numerous books, including *The Phenomenology of Mind*, *Science of Logic*, *Philosophy of Right*, *Philosophy of History*, and *Philosophy of Religion*. However, if we look deeper into his basic thinking, we find that it can be condensed under three titles: the Hegelian Dialectic, which is the law of world movements; the absolute spirit, which was the name of God; and the state, in which he showed a keen interest.

Some later scholars have criticized Hegel's philosophy as not being a "philosophy of man." They claim that his philosophy is that of the non-human or superman; they find the idea of God residing inside man and being responsible for all thought as somehow dehumanizing. However, this is only because they do not know the truth that we are all children of Buddha and that the world is run according to a plan devised by the high spirits. It is only the stupid talk of mediocre scholars who know no better. Hegel was indeed the reincarnation of Plato, and this was reflected in the fact that he had lifelong admiration for the Greek spirit and thought that the ideal form for communities to take would be to re-adopt that of the Greek "polis."

8. The Fall to Atheism

It can be said that German idealistic philosophy came to an end with Hegel. This was because Hegel's intuitive understanding of the speculative form of God was beyond the understanding of both his contemporaries and those who were to come later. To Hegel, the aim of philosophy was to grasp the ultimate truth of the ideal. According to his own philosophy, it was possible for man to raise himself up to the level of God. This is the thinking of a man who had reached the heights of enlightenment in a philosophical sense and it was impossible for ordinary scholars to follow his reasoning.

It is hardly surprising, therefore, that no sooner had Hegel died than a movement began that criticized his work. First there was the "Hegelian Youth" movement, then David Strauss (1808–1874), who denied the supernatural elements of the gospels, putting them down as mere myths in his *Life of Jesus* that was published in 1835. Bruno Bauer (1809–1882) took Hegel's famous dictum "the real is rational" and interpreted it as meaning "the real has to be rational and reasonable," adopting the radical and revolutionary idea that anything irrational should be eradicated from reality. It can be said that the members of the "Hegelian Youth" movement were to have a strong ideological influence over Marx. Unfortunately, however, this represents a fall from the ideological heights that had been reached by Hegel.

Both Karl Marx (1818–1883) and the positivist Auguste Comte (1798–1857) were high spirits sent from heaven to instigate a practical social revolution. First, Thomas More and the utopian thinkers had been sent to instill in the people on Earth a picture of the ideal land, then Kant, Hegel, and the other idealists came to present an intellectual view of the Truth that would be acceptable to modern and contemporary society. The next step in order to transcend the two preceding movements and further the utopianization of a society based on philosophy was to send Karl Marx, Friedrich Engels (1820–1895), Auguste Comte, and

Herbert Spencer (1820–1903), whose role was to create the ideal contemporary society as quickly as possible.

I would like to take this opportunity to talk on Karl Marx's earlier incarnations. In his former life, he was born on the island of Samos to an immigrant from Athens and went by the name Epicurus (341–270 B.C.). Epicurus became the founder of the system known as Epicureanism. He preached a form of materialism after the model of Democritus, saying that all matter comprised atoms. Plato maintained that man had an immortal soul and was most emphatic about the subject in his book *Phaedo*. But Epicurus took the opposite position, saying that humans perished through the decomposition of their bodily atoms and, therefore, it was illogical to fear death as a punishment. Neither did Epicurus agree with Plato's theory of an ideal state run by a philosopher-king, saying that no intelligent person would want anything to do with politics any more than they would want to rule. This kind of ideological criticism is typical of the kind of thing he liked to say when he was reincarnated as Karl Marx two thousand years later.

Indeed, fate is an ironic thing. In ancient Greece, Epicurus preached hedonism and criticized Plato for his beliefs, and when Plato was reincarnated as Hegel, Epicurus in his incarnation as Marx used historical materialism to lambaste him once more. It is said that history repeats itself and the same is true of human relationships in their various reincarnations. However, in the same way that Plato was a far greater man than Epicurus, Hegel also

towered over Marx, as future history will clearly show. The
way in which people such as Plato or Hegel, who preach the
philosophy of Truth, are always followed by those who
preach materialism is not just a paradox, it is a test for those
of us living in the world.

As a result of his materialistic philosophy while living
on Earth, Epicurus, after he died, was banished to the
Unconscious Hell (where the souls wander unconscious
even of their own death) and suffered for a period of two
hundred years. The same is true of Marx. He died in 1883,
which is a little over one hundred years ago, but he is still a
captive in the Unconscious Hell. He will not be released
until China undergoes a democratic revolution, which is
expected to happen within the next few decades following
the disintegration of the Soviet Union. In the final analysis,
Marx's philosophy is nothing more than a persecution
complex that claims that society alienates the people, with
at its base a profound envy of Hegel (Plato), which dates
back to Marx's former life as Epicurus. However, despite
Marx's failings as a human, his underlying desire to create
an ideal society on Earth demonstrates that he came originally from the Bodhisattva Realm.

9. The Dance of the Dwarfs

The success of Marx's philosophy exceeded even his expectations and was to spread far and wide. His thoughts were to
lead directly to the destruction of Tsarist Russia, the
creation of the Union of Soviet Socialist Republics, and,

eventually, the formation of the People's Republic of China. Despite the great spread of Idealism during the eighteenth and nineteenth centuries, materialistic atheism suddenly came into ascendancy and it looked as if nothing would stop it from spreading over the entire globe. However, various failings became evident in the communist countries.

First, contrary to Marx's expectations, the formation of a proletarian dictatorship did not occur. Instead, both the Soviet Union and China saw the creation of a new privileged elite who held all the power, while the common people were all equal only in their poverty. In other words, far from creating a utopian communist society, all communism did was produce a new ruling class, while the average citizens were forced to live equally in poverty.

The second problem with communism was that it created a reign of terror. Purge followed purge, political differences were solved through violence. Everywhere was war and destruction; it was hell manifest in this world on Earth. There are any number of criteria by which a country may be judged, and it is quite possible that from the communists' point of view, the free countries of the world may appear to languish under military imperialism. However, there are very few political refugees who defect from the West while there is a never-ending flow in the opposite direction. How can this be explained? Whichever way it is looked at, a country whose citizens think only of escape must be an evil country.

The third failing of communism is shown in the policy of ignorance that is invariably adopted by the government. When I talk of an ignorance policy, I am referring to the thought control that kills the individual's conscience, the absence of freedom of speech, and a lack of freedom of the press that can only lead to ignorance in the majority of the population. Utopian communism should have created a communal society of truly free and cultured people, not an egalitarian nation of chained slaves—in other words, the atheist countries that have appeared since Marx have dragged people down from their position as children of Buddha and recreated them as machines whose only value lies in their ability to provide labor.

One extreme example of this kind of thinking can be seen in the theory of evolution as laid out by Charles Darwin (1809–1882) in his book *The Origin of Species*. In this, humankind is reduced to an accident of nature resulting from the chance evolution of amebas. Darwin was not a hypocritical man and, having realized how his mistaken theories had led to the spread of atheism, his conscience would give him no peace. He is now serving a penance in Abysmal Hell. While freedom of thought and freedom of speech are important, it is a sin to publicize ideas or words that will lead others astray—a sin that can only be atoned for by the person who committed it. Who else could put things right? The fact that materialism is a false philosophy becomes obvious the minute you return to the Real World, and it is in an effort to dispel such mistaken teachings that I am writing this book. What I want you to understand is that the history of the human race is not the result of a series of accidents, nor the consequence of trial and error by human beings as animals. It is all part of a master plan created by the high spirits in heaven.

Pretending to be a giant of philosophy, Friedrich Nietzsche (1844–1900) proclaimed "God is dead," and when he returned to the Real World he was met by the derision of the myriad spirits. Adolf Hitler (1889–1945) tried to put Nietzsche's thought into practice and promote a super-race, and provoked the Second World War. They are both now languishing in the quagmire of the deepest realm of hell, their limbs shackled with chains and balls of steel. The giants of this world are the dwarfs of the next. They suffer in the darkest realms of hell, while the simple farmer who lived his life with a naive faith finds his reward in heaven. The most important thing in this world is not power or intellectual knowledge; it is a belief in Buddha and an understanding of the spirit world. It is only once this has been attained that one is able to think about right faith. It is important that people realize this and open their eyes to the truth as soon as possible.

Although Lenin's ideology when he led the Bolshevik revolution was mistaken, he was motivated by a strong desire to help the people of Russia and, therefore, he lives today in a village for politicians in the Realm of the Good in the fifth dimension. Stalin, on the other hand, is banished to deepest hell until he is forgiven by the victims of the purges he instigated. The good deeds and thoughts of Mao Tse-tung slightly outweigh the evil ones and, therefore, he too is now a resident of the Realm of the Good in the fifth dimension, although the errors in his ideology will continue to be revealed in the course of time.

10. Tearing Away Twentieth Century Thought

I would like now to have a broad picture of the twentieth century and pick out a few thinkers who embodied the Truth in their work. I will begin by looking at the existentialist movement.

Existentialism originated with the Danish philosopher, Søren Kierkegaard (1813–1855). His philosophy, as explained in his works *The Sickness Unto Death*, *Either/Or*, and *The Concept of Dread*, is based on a realization of the uncertainty of life. In a way, this could also be taken as meaning the impermanence of life. In this respect, some may find that it has a lot in common with Buddhist philosophy.

Existentialism's affinity with Buddhism is hardly surprising when one realizes that in a previous life, Kierkegaard was Asanga (c.310–c.390), who with his brother Vasubandhu worked to bring Mahayana Buddhism to its prime. When talking of the different stages of life, Kierkegaard refers to the aesthetic stage, the ethical stage, and the religious stage, and this kind of thinking is very reminiscent of the teachings of Theravada Buddhism, which aims at the perfection of the self. Existentialism, as a contemporary philosophy dealing with human existence that has been thrown into this world, forms a defined philosophical movement during the twentieth century.

First we see the German, Karl Jaspers (1883–1969), who is most famous for his works *Philosophy*, *Man in the Modern Age*, and *Reason and Existence*. At heart, his philosophy can be summed up under two categories. Firstly, he says that one's "authentic self" can only be established during extreme situations or what he describes as "boundary situations." Secondly, he says that through the interaction with a transcendental being one can transcend all the limitations imposed by reality and attain true freedom of being. In the same way that Kierkegaard was from the Bodhisattva Realm and a reincarnation of Asanga, Jaspers was the Chinese Buddhist, I Ching (635–713), who brought numerous sutras back with him after traveling to India. He later wrote a book about his journey, which was called *To the Southern Sea and Back in Search of the Law*, and is now a resident of the Brahma Realm, the highest part of the Bodhisattva Realm.

Another philosopher of the existentialist movement was Martin Heidegger (1889–1976), who is said to be the greatest philosopher of the twentieth century. He was a reincarnation of St. Augustine (354–430), a Christian scholar of the late Roman era and an inhabitant now of the Tathagata Realm. If there are any among you who would like to check for yourselves that Heidegger really was a reincarnation of St. Augustine, just compare his work,

Being and Time, to Augustine's theory of time and you should be left in no doubt whatsoever.

The Tathagata Heidegger considered man as "being-in-the-world" (Dasein) and said that we are thrown into the possibilities of everyday life, but can project ourselves into future possibilities ("thrown projection"). However, this philosophy does not go far beyond the discussion of fatalism and self-power, and he has been criticized by Hegel in heaven for not being more precise about the existence of the kingdom of God or the Real World that exists in the fourth dimension and beyond.

Next comes Jean-Paul Sartre (1905–1980), who was born in France. Sartre is originally from the Realm of Light in the sixth dimension. His form of existentialism separates human beings from the existence of objects (being in itself), in that we can make and transcend ourselves (being for itself). However, this degree of enlightenment may seem a little primitive to somebody who has already awoken to the Truth. It is a pity that Sartre did not spend a little more time studying Buddha's creation of the world and humankind, or the fact that humans are all the children of Buddha.

Another flow of ideas in the twentieth century stemmed from pragmatism, and one of the most famous proponents of this philosophy was the American William James (1842–1910). His ideas are demonstrated in his book *Pragmatism*. They can be summed up in the phrase, "Since it is true, it is useful and since it is useful, it is true." Unfortunately, however, this philosophy is only relevant in the evolution of this world; looked at from an understanding of the entire Truth, it can be said to represent the enlightenment and philosophy of the Realm of Light. William James has returned to the upper reaches of the Realm of Light in the sixth dimension. Another pragmatist was John Dewey (1859–1952). Dewey stated that man is an organic entity and the world is nothing more than the environment he lives in, and that man's intellectual activities, his knowledge, theories, ideas etc. are merely tools he uses to adapt himself to this environment. His philosophy is called instrumentalism. In other words, Dewey brought ideas down from the abstract to a realistic, commonplace level. One reason why he preached this form of experimentalism is that he was influenced by Darwin's materialism. Dewey's soul lives in lower area of the Realm of Light.

Twentieth-century philosophy, be it existentialism or pragmatism, has had the effect of lowering humans from their position as children of Buddha, making them blind and insecure, and interested only in material gain. We must overcome this trend and return to those philosophies that are based on the Truth. To this end, I intend to establish a philosophy of the Truth.

Chapter Three
Eternal Mountains and Rivers

1. The Origins of Oriental Thought

In Chapter Two, I outlined the main stream of Western philosophical thought. The chapter was also a description of a history of the high spirits who were incarnated in the Western world. While it is impossible for me to describe all the activities of these high spirits, I think I have succeeded in summing up the main points.

In this chapter, I would like to move on and take a look at the activities of the high spirits or the Great Guiding Spirits of Light within Eastern history. In other words, I will be looking at Eastern history from the viewpoint of the Real World, and in so doing show that Buddha never deserted us but has continually sent numerous high spirits down to live with us, to lead the evolution and development of life on Earth.

Oriental thought can be divided into two main streams, one originating in India and the other in China, and I would like to start by discussing that of India. There are some areas in the world that are very highly charged with spiritual magnetism, while others are not. India is obviously one of the former; over the last few thousand years it has been a highly spiritual land, emitting a powerful light.

The first spiritual leader to appear in this land was Vishnu, who was born in approximately 6500 B.C. and was later worshipped as a god. Vishnu is the god of love and wisdom and comes originally from the Tathagata Realm.

In approximately 4700 B.C. a man called Silvananda was born in western India. His life was to form the basis of the legend of the god Shiva. Shiva is known as the god of destruction and Silvananda was, in fact, a brilliant military hero who was later to be reincarnated as Alexander the Great (356–323 B.C.). In this later life, he studied philosophy under Aristotle, then went on to conquer the Greek cities and Persia and beyond, almost as far as India, building cities in various lands that he named after himself, raising the curtain on the age of Hellenism. Among the great politicians and generals who have appeared in history, there are some Great Guiding Spirits of Light who have come to Earth with the aim of creating a new age in accordance with Buddha's plans. Shiva, who was also Alexander, was an inhabitant of the Tathagata Realm and still later he was to be incarnated in Corsica as Napoleon Bonaparte (1769–1821). In this life, he became a hero in both the battlefield and politics, instituting the Napoleonic Code and becoming the first emperor of France. In the Real World, he is known as the god of freedom.

The third great spirit to become incarnate in India was Krishna. Krishna is mentioned in the ancient poem about the gods called the *Bhagavad Gita* and his teachings were based around trust, love, and affection. He was born around 4700 B.C. and was later reincarnated in Egypt as Clario, who taught laws and bolstered the national feeling of the people. Finally, he was born as Jesus of Nazareth in 4 B.C. a grand Tathagata of the ninth dimension.

The ideas of these great people were later recorded in the eighth century B.C. in a book called the *Rig Veda*. They were added to in the seventh century B.C. by the *Upanishads*. A major teaching in these books is that the ultimate reality of the universe, which they call Brahma, and the self, which is called the Atman, are originally one and the same thing. Brahma is a Guiding Spirit of Light who is on the threshold of the realm of the Tathagata. This was considered the same as godliness and it was thought that this divine nature dwelled within all human beings. This idea was later developed in Buddhism, which claims that it is possible to attain enlightenment through disciplining of the mind and become a buddha (an enlightened being).

Next I would like to talk about China. The first great leader there was Yao (T'ao-t'ang-tze) who was born in Shansi in around 3200 B.C. After becoming emperor, Yao founded an ideal theocracy and as a result his fame spread throughout the land. His spirit came originally from the Tathagata Realm and he was later reincarnated as Akbar the Great (1542–1605), the man who founded the Mogul

Empire in India. He created the golden era of this empire, organizing the army and bureaucracy, abolishing the head tax (called Jizya), and trying to reconcile Islam and Hinduism. He also tried to create a new religion called Din Ilahi (Divine Faith), but in this he was unsuccessful.

Yao did not leave his kingdom to his son, but rather abdicated in favor of Shun, a man who was renowned for his filial devotion and wisdom. Shun was later reincarnated as Emperor Wu-ti (159–87 B.C.) of the Han dynasty, who enlarged the empire and established a centralized government. Shun was also from the Tathagata Realm and was reincarnated in more recent history in America as President Franklin D. Roosevelt (1882–1945). During this lifetime, he worked to bring about a recovery from the Great Depression of the 1930s through his New Deal policies.

Shun passed the crown on to Yu, a man of great virtue and an expert at flood control. Yu went on to create the country of Hsia and was a spirit from the upper Bodhisattva Realm. He was later reincarnated as Emperor Justinian I (483–565) of the Byzantine Empire who ordered his chief legal advisor, Tribonian, to revise and edit the existing laws to create the *Corpus Juris Civilis*, which represented the sum of Roman law and which was to have a profound influence on early European law. He was reincarnated yet again as Jawaharlal Nehru (1889–1964), who was to become the first prime minister of India after it received independence following the Second World War.

2. Buddhism and Jainism

I have already explained that the gods Vishnu, Shiva, and Krishna were very powerful in the theology of ancient India and their teachings are summed up in the sacred Indian scriptures known as the Vedas. The highest class in Indian society is the Brahmin and it became their task to undertake priestly duties in accordance with the Vedas. The caste system has a very long history in India, and was already in place over two thousand years ago. Basically, the population was divided into four categories: the Brahmin (priests), the Kshatriya (warriors and rulers), the Vaisya (commoners engaged in agriculture, industry and commerce), and the Sudra (menial laborers). [See Author's Note 1, p. 217]

Popular belief had it that the Buddha (the enlightened or awakened one) would appear among the Brahmin class as prophesied in the Vedas, but Gautama Siddhartha (Shakyamuni) was born to the Kshatriya class. As a result, he suffered from persecution by the Brahmins after he renounced a secular life and attained enlightenment.

There is disagreement among scholars as to when exactly Shakyamuni lived; some put his birth at 566 B.C., others claim that it was 563 or 463 B.C., while the Akashic Records in the Real World put his birth even earlier. The Buddhists of southern Asia believe he was born in 624 B.C. and entered Nirvana in 544 B.C.. Consequently, the Buddhists of Sri Lanka, India, Myanmar, Thailand, Laos, and Cambodia held special services in 1956/57 to celebrate the two thousand five hundredth anniversary of his entry into Nirvana. Incidentally, 1956 was the same year that I was reincarnated in Japan. Shakyamuni was born in Kapilavastu in the country of Kosala (present-day Nepal) as a prince of the Shakya clan, but I will return to discuss his teachings in detail later on.

Another member of the Kshatriya class who was to become a religious leader was Vardhamana (usually known by his honorific name of Mahavira), who started Jainism. He denied the authority of the Brahmins, saying that the only way to salvation was through asceticism. The most notable feature of his faith is the strict injunction not to kill any form of life and a complicated system of rules to ensure this. Whereas Buddhism won converts in the Brahmin, Kshatriya, and Vaisya classes, Jainism found most of its supporters among the Vaisyas and was to have a strong influence on Hinduism. Mahavira is an inhabitant of the Minor Heaven.

At approximately the same time, a group of free thinkers appeared in India who also denied the authority of Brahmanism. Ajita produced a materialistic theory, claiming that only the four elements—earth, water, fire, and wind—truly existed. He was later reincarnated as Roger Bacon (1214–1294), a Franciscan monk and thinker who renounced Scholasticism and introduced empiricism into philosophy, thus calling forth the age of modern science.

Pakudha added pain, pleasure, and life to the four elements propounded by Ajita, producing a total of seven elements. Another thinker, Purana, denied the concept of morality, saying that there was no such thing as good or evil deeds. To mention one final Indian philosopher from this period, we have Sanjaya. He was a great skeptic and, no matter what he was asked, he refused to give a clear answer. This resulted in his being known as the "eel polemicist." He was later reincarnated as the British skeptic and positivist David Hume (1711–1776), and is a resident of the upper reaches of the Light Realm.

3. Shakyamuni's Buddhism as a Philosophy (1)

I would like now to consider the teachings of Shakyamuni Buddha, which are sometimes referred to as "The Light of Asia," from a philosophical point of view. So rich and varied was Shakyamuni's teaching that it is said that it contains eighty-four thousand gates to the Law, and this diversity makes it a source of endless wonder. However, the main pillars of Shakyamuni's teachings can be summarized under the following five points.

The first pillar is the relationship between the Real World and this world, by which I mean the three-dimensional phenomenal world. Shakyamuni referred to this frequently. The following is what he would teach:

The Real World is an eternal realm where human souls exist both before birth and after death, whereas the three-dimensional world is nothing more than a temporary abode. The Real World was created through the will of the Primordial Buddha[1] (the Creator), while the three-dimensional

---

1. Refer to *The Laws of the Sun*, Chapter 1: The Light of Cosmic Consciousness.

world is simply a reflection of this, so what we think of as the world is nothing more than a shadow picture. Unfortunately, the majority of people believe that this shadow world, this temporary abode, is the only world that exists and they cling to it desperately, bringing upon themselves much misery. In order to escape from this anguish, it is necessary to remember the Real World where we all originated, to cast off our attachment to our material selves and find our true selves. If we succeed in this we can cast aside the sufferings of birth, aging, and illness. All that will remain is a world of joy as we become dazzling manifestations of light. This is the first thing that you have to learn.

The second pillar of his teaching is the theory of time. If the first precept is taken to be the theory of space, the second lies in the concept of temporal causation. The law of cause and effect runs through both the phenomenal world and the Real World, joining one action to the next and one person to another. It is the relationship that gives birth to everything in the universe. Human beings are subject to the law of reincarnation in the eternal flow of time, and reincarnation in turn is governed by the law of cause and effect.

What kind of world and what kind of life we will experience after death depends entirely on our life in the present world in the same way that our present spiritual leanings and surroundings were dictated by our past existences. To put it another way, if we live a perfect life in this world, we will be assured of a splendid existence in the next. Therefore, in order to break out of the vicious circle of destiny, we have no choice but to devote ourselves to good and rebuild our lives, which until now have been left to the whims of fate. This is what is meant by emancipation. To discover our true self, which is adamantine and immune to the vagaries of fate, is to discover enlightenment. Moreover, if we achieve the state of Tathagata through enlightenment, our reincarnation will cease to be ruled by the law of causality and it will become possible for us to be reborn through our own free will. This is the second pillar of Shakyamuni's philosophy.

The third pillar of Shakyamuni's teachings is the so-called "Noble Eightfold Path." This represents the road to human perfection and provides a yardstick by which to measure our personal spiritual development. When people are born as babies in this world, they forget everything about the Real World and have to live with only a surface consciousness, the bulk of their knowledge being hidden in their subconscious. The only way that people catch a glimpse of the true consciousness that they left behind in the Real World is through what we refer to as inspiration, or in their personal spiritual leanings. Worldly desires that spring from a life centered around physical values are what separate our surface consciousness from our subconscious. Until we are capable of ridding ourselves of these desires, we will never be able to find our true self, to regain one hundred percent of our latent capabilities. Worldly desires are negative mental functions, formed since birth by the distorted environment, education, thoughts, beliefs, habits, disharmony, and guilty actions. Therefore, it is important for us to look back over our lives, up to the present day, to contemplate the reasons for the disharmony that exist in our hearts and minds, and then repent of them one by one. The criteria we should use for this introspection are laid down in the Noble Eightfold Path, which is comprised of the eight right ways.

First you must consider whether you have really seen the incidents you have experienced and the people whose destinies have crossed your own—seen, that is, from the viewpoint of right religious faith. (Right View)

Next, have your thoughts been pure? This is very important. Have your thoughts been unruly, disarrayed, or impure? If your mind were transparent, is there nothing in it that you would be ashamed of other people seeing? (Right Thought)

The next question to put to yourself is: Have you always spoken the right words? One of the main causes of people's suffering is the casual words of others, spoken without thinking, or bad remarks we regret uttering ourselves. Does this apply to you or have you really always spoken appropriately? (Right Speech)

Have you always acted rightly and devoted yourself to your job? A job is something Buddha gives us to become a service of gratitude and it is a vocation, but are you really fulfilling your calling? (Right Action)

Have you lived rightly? Do you consider your life in this world a time of training and do you live each day fully as if it were your whole life? Have you lived a life of harmony, with the Truth as food for your soul? (Right Livelihood)

Have you made the effort to travel the right path? Are you sure that you have not lost your way as a child of Buddha? Have you never neglected your studies of the Truth but always striven to improve yourself? (Right Effort)

Next we come to Right Mindfulness. Have you made an appropriate plan for your life? Have you prayed rightly to Buddha? Are you always striving to achieve self-realization so that you would not be ashamed to appear before Buddha Himself? (Right Mindfulness)

Finally, we come to Right Concentration. Have you managed to reach a true state of spiritual concentration through meditation? The true object of meditation is not to think nothing, but rather to receive the light of Buddha from the Real World and gain the guidance of your guardian and guiding spirits. This is an indispensable form of study for all those who would seek the way to the Truth. (Right Concentration)

In this way, the third pillar teaches people to reflect on their past while building an ideal future based on the Noble Eightfold Path.

4. Shakyamuni's Buddhism as a Philosophy (2)

The fourth pillar of Shakyamuni's teachings is that bene-fiting the self can benefit others. This is expressed in the so-called philosophy of the "Six Paramitas," or six perfections. The Sanskrit word "parami" means inherent wisdom, while "ta" refers to the way this wisdom overflows. The Six Paramitas are as follows:

1. *Dana-paramita*

   This is the perfection of offering or charity, which is the earthly manifestation of mercy. It refers to the material and spiritual charity that people offer to others in an effort to save them. This concept has something in common with the Christian idea of love.

2. *Sila-paramita*

   This is the perfection of observing the precepts. It refers to the five Buddhist precepts: Do not kill, do not steal, do not commit adultery, do not speak falsely, and do not drink to the extent that your life is ruined.

3. *Ksanti-paramita*

   This is the perfection of perseverance. If other people say antagonistic things or vent their anger on you, and you react by becoming angry yourself, you do not qualify as a seeker of the Truth. Even though it may be the other person's fault, once you have taken in the poison yourself, you will be attuned to the vibrations of hell. On the other hand, if you remain calm and let them go their own way, other people's abuse, jealousy, or anger will simply return to them. This is what is known as the law of action and reaction.

4. *Virya-paramita*

   This is the perfection of effort. Of course, this refers to the efforts of the seeker to understand and practice the Truth, which should be built up on a daily basis.

5. *Dhyana-paramita*

   This is the perfection of meditation and its aim is to achieve communication with the Real World.

6. *Prajna-paramita*

   This is the perfection of wisdom, which lies at the very heart of Shakyamuni's teachings. His light is the light of wisdom that shines with a golden hue. In other words, Shakyamuni Buddha is the Guiding Spirit of Light whose task is to explain the whole picture and system of the Law in an intellectual way. He is the one who holds the key to the treasure house of wisdom in the Real World.

The Six Paramitas I have listed here represent a teaching whose goal is to uplift the self while improving our relationship with others. At the same time, the teaching explains that by aiming to achieve these six perfections, we are able to attain enlightenment. The Six Paramitas are similar in content to the Noble Eightfold Path, and in some areas the two teachings overlap. The Noble Eightfold Path represents a method of training to become an Arhat, that is to say, to arrive at the threshold of the Bodhisattva state, whereas the Six Paramitas show the way to advance from the Bodhisattva to the Tathagata states.

Some people consider that the Noble Eightfold Path belongs mainly to the Theravada or "Lesser Vehicle" Buddhism while the Six Paramitas belong mainly to the Mahayana or "Great Vehicle" Buddhism. In fact, however, the two teachings differ simply in that they aim to achieve different levels of enlightenment. You cannot become a Bodhisattva without understanding the "love that gives" any more than you can become a Tathagata without having awakened to wisdom. Both love and wisdom are necessary to be Tathagata.

The fifth pillar of Shakyamuni's teachings is the concept of the "void" (Sanskrit: *shūnyatā*; Japanese: *kū*). The meaning of the Buddhist teaching of the void has been a constant topic of discussion for over two thousand years. What is the meaning of this void that is quoted in the famous Buddhist expression "matter is void, void is matter"? It is what I referred to in the second thesis of the "Physics of the Light of Buddha" in Section 3 of Chapter One—creation and destruction occur through the process of condensation or diffusion of Buddha's Light.

In the Real World of the fourth dimension and above, if the Light of Buddha is condensed for a specific purpose, a spiritual entity will appear. This spiritual entity has a certain wavelength and, if this is further condensed, it will appear in the third dimension as a material object. This means that all the material objects that we see in this world actually comprise condensed particles of the Light of Buddha that are held in place through the power of spiritual energy focused with an explicit intention, or will. It also follows that once this will is extinguished, the material objects of this world will revert to their original form as particles of light. So do these particles of light actually exist? No, they do not. These particles, otherwise known as photons, are created through the energy of Buddha's will being focused on a particular spot. If His will were extinguished, these photons would cease to exist. In the three-dimensional world, photons gather with a particular purpose—to create atoms, which in turn form molecules that cluster together to produce particles that are the basic building blocks of all matter. Therefore, if the Light of Buddha was removed, it would mean the end of both the phenomenal world of the third dimension as well as the Real World of the fourth dimension and above.

This is the true meaning of the expression "matter is void, void is matter." What we think of as the world can be broken down into photons and these photons are the manifestation of the will of Buddha, and so nothing actually exists. However, these originally nonexistent photons have been compressed to create spiritons, then protons, atoms, molecules, and particles, which in turn combine to create matter. This is the true meaning of Shakyamuni Buddha's concept of the void.

5. The Flow of Buddha's Wisdom

There are countless teachings of Shakyamuni Buddha other than the ones I have talked about here, and a more comprehensive discussion of them may be found in some of my other books.

Shakyamuni left this world shortly before his eighty-first birthday. It was in April by the Gregorian calendar and the weather was unusually good. As he finally passed on, all life, both animal and plant, joined in mourning. Shortly after his death, five hundred of his pupils who had reached the state of Arhat joined together at Rajagrha, the capital of Magadha, to set down the teachings of their master for posterity. This was known as the First Council and the practice was repeated several times over the next four hundred years.

However, after several hundred years, the true meaning of the teachings of Shakyamuni Buddha became diluted. In order to rectify this situation, Nagarjuna was sent down to India from the Real World in around the second century A.D.. Nagarjuna was a spirit of the Tathagata Realm and his mission on Earth was very similar to the one entrusted to Martin Luther in the Christian Church. Nagarjuna is said to be the founder of the Madhyamika sect of Mahayana Buddhism and, as can be seen from his two books, *On Great Wisdom* and *The Middle Doctrine*, his philosophy is built on two main points. First, there is the idea that Buddha's teachings should be systematized in an orderly fashion to facilitate their transmission to future generations.

Second, he was strongly influenced, while he was still living in the Real World, by the Christian concept of love, and he translated this into a Buddhist philosophy, founding the Mahayana branch of Buddhism in an effort to save all living beings.

One of Nagarjuna's successors was named Deba, a spirit from the upper reaches of the Bodhisattva Realm. After finishing his mission in third-century India, he was then reincarnated in Japan as the priest Honen (1133–1212) and founded the Nembutsu form of worship (the repeated chanting of the name of Amida Buddha or Amitabha).

India next saw the appearance of two brothers, Asanga (c.310–c.390) and Vasubandhu (c.320–c.400), who brought Mahayana Buddhism to its peak. Asanga was later reincarnated in Europe as the existentialist philosopher Søren Kierkegaard, whom I described in Chapter Two. Vasubandhu, who was also from the Bodhisattva Realm, was reincarnated in China as Lu Hsiang-shan (Lu Chiu-yuan) (1139–1192) in the Sung dynasty. Lu Hsiang-shan was a famous scholar who supported spiritualism in opposition to Chu Hsi, and this spiritualism was to become one of the main themes of the Wang Yang-ming school of Confucianism that flourished during the Ming dynasty. After the death of these two brothers, however, Buddhism began to go into decline in its native India.

6. And Buddhism Flows into China

As Buddhism declined in India its center moved to China. The teachings of Nagarjuna were handed down through

Hui-wen and Hui-ssu (515–577) of the Northern Ch'i period to Chih-i, one of Hui-ssu's disciples. Both Hui-wen and Hui-ssu came from the Bodhisattva Realm. However, it was T'ien-t'ai Chih-i (538–597) who brought Buddhism to prominence in China. So great was his standing, that he was personally appointed by the Sui Emperor, Yang-ti, and awarded the honorific title of Master Chih-che (Great Teacher of Wisdom). His teachings were based on the Lotus Sutra and their analytical and systematic content made them very original.

One morning, in his thirty-ninth year, T'ien-t'ai Chih-i had a dream shortly before dawn in which he saw a vision of Shakyamuni Buddha, flanked on either side by the Manjushri Bodhisattva and Samantabhadra Bodhisattva. Buddha beckoned to him and spoke, saying, "Chih-i, today I will teach you the secret of the world within, and I want you to transmit this knowledge to all the future generations of the world." This was the origin of what was to become known as the doctrine of "one thought leads to three thousand worlds."

T'ien-t'ai continued to receive instruction from Shakyamuni on numerous occasions until he attained true enlightenment and was able to communicate freely with the spirit world. By 594, when he preached his *Discourse on Mahayana Meditation and Contemplation*, he had already arrived at the full enlightenment of the Tathagata.

The teachings of T'ien-t'ai Chih-i were first introduced into Japan by Chien-chen (688–763) in 753, but they did not meet with much success. However, that was not the end, and in 804, a Japanese priest named Saicho went to China and studied the innermost secrets of the creed before returning to Japan the following year to spread the knowledge he had gained. The sect was further popularized through the efforts of the priests Enchin and Ennin.

A new doctrine to appear in China was Zen (Chan in Chinese) Buddhism, which was introduced from India by Bodhidharma (446–528). Bodhidharma had been born a prince of a royal family in southern India, but so eager was he to spread the word that at the age of fifty-six he traveled by ship to China and began to preach in the area around Loyang. He is famous for having sat facing a wall in meditation at the Shaolin temple for nine years.

Bodhidharma was reincarnated in Japan in recent years as Daisetsu Suzuki (1870–1966), whose work in spreading Zen in the West bears a lot in common with Bodhidharmas's earlier work in China. Bodhidharma was originally from the Bodhisattva Realm, but fell during his life as Daisetsu Suzuki when he became too involved in academic intellectualism, and for that reason he is now undergoing training in the upper area of the Light Realm.

The second founder of the Zen sect in China was Huiko (487–593), who began by studying Confucian and Taoist philosophy but then later became one of Bodhidharma's students. There is a famous legend that despite Hui-ko's pleas, Bodhidharma would not teach him and so, one snowy night, he cut off his own arm at the elbow and offered it to

Bodhidharma to demonstrate the depth of his desire to learn. However, this is an exaggeration; the truth of the story is that, having been refused, Hui-ko cut his elbow with a sword and used the blood that flowed from the wound to write a letter to Bodhidharma, pleading to become his disciple.

Another famous Zen priest was Hui-kai (1183–1260), who wrote *The Gateless Barrier.* He was born seventeen years earlier than Dogen (1200–1253) and, as I mentioned earlier, was a reincarnation of Aristotle who was later reborn as Kitaro Nishida.

Esoteric Buddhism first made an appearance in China in 716, when Subhakarasimha (637–735) brought the teachings with him from eastern India and was favorably received by Emperor Hsuantzung. He lived in Hsi-ming temple, where he devoted himself to translating esoteric scriptures, and he is particularly famous for his Chinese translation of the Mahavairocana Sutra. He was later reincarnated in Japan as Nichiro (1243–1320), one of Nichiren's six elder disciples.

Another priest of esoteric Buddhism who was active at approximately the same time as Subhakarasimha was Vajrabodhi (669–741). He was from southern India and after studying esoteric Buddhism under Nagabodhi, he went to Chang-an in 720 and began to preach. I-hang (683–727) was a famous priest who studied under both Subhakarasimha and Vajrabodhi.

Amoghavajra (705–774) was a priest who studied under Vajrabodhi in Lo-yang, then traveled to Ceylon (present-day Sri Lanka) in 741 to study under Nagabodhi before returning in 746 to China where he translated the Diamond Peak Sutra and other Buddhist literature. One of his disciples, Hui-kuo (746–805), went on to teach the famous Japanese monk Kukai. Subhakarasimha and Amoghavajra were Brahma while Vajrabodhi, I-hang, and Hui-kuo were Bodhisattva.

7. Going Back to Confucius

So far we have looked at the spread of Buddhism in China, but this country also spawned its own unique philosophies—Confucianism and Taoism. I will start by looking at the life and teachings of Confucius (552–479 B.C.). He was born in Lu (now Shantung province) and studied hard until he reached the position of Minister of Justice in his home state. He did not remain in this office for long, however, and after a few years he began to travel around the neighboring provinces of Wei, Ch'en, Sung, Chong, Tsai, and T'su, preaching the Way. In his later years, he returned to his home state where he devoted himself to editing scriptures and teaching. At the heart of his teaching lie his views on the way to human perfection and the ideal state.

Confucius comes from the Cosmic Realm of the ninth dimension, putting him on the same level as Shakyamuni Buddha, Jesus Christ, or Moses. However, unlike his fellow spirits, he did not talk much about heaven, although this was not due to ignorance. He was thoroughly versed in the affairs of the Real World.

Why should it be that the collection of Confucius' sayings, *Lun-yu* (The Analects of Confucius), has been read continuously for twenty-five hundred years and why does it still have the power to move people's minds and hearts? It is because his words are words of Light, the words of the Truth. When we look among his writings, we can find many instances where they contain the words of Guiding Spirits of Light. An example of this is when his disciple Tzu-kung asked him, "Is there any single word that can act as a principle for the rest of our lives?" Confucius replied, "Consideration. Do not do to others as you would not want others to do to you." It is easy to see that this concept is extremely close to that expounded by Jesus Christ.

Again, when Confucius' leading disciple Yen-hui asked him the meaning of "Jen" (perfect virtue), he replied, "What makes Jen is the mastery over self and the return to "Li" (propriety, civility)." When Yen-hui asked how this could be achieved, Confucius replied, "Do not look upon that which is not proper, do not listen to that which is not proper, do not say that which is not proper, and do not move if it is not proper." This particular teaching holds a lot in common with that put forward by the Japanese Shinto gods, including Amaterasu-O-Mikami (the Sun Goddess) and Ame-no-Minakanushi-no-Kami (God Ruling the Center of Heaven). Confucius believed that music had the power to ease people's hearts and nurture their noble sentiments. This insight about the power of music was sent from ancient Greek gods, Hermes and Zeus, in heaven. With regard to his political ideas, Confucius is reported in the Analects as saying: "If you administer the affairs of state with virtue, you will become like the north star, you will remain stationary and all other stars will look toward you." As can be seen from this, Confucius supported the idea of righteous government by a virtuous king and this teaching, too, agrees with that of the Japanese Shinto gods.

Mencius (c.372–289 B.C.) adopted the principle of righteous government and combined it with the idea of human nature's fundamental good. He followed the teachings of Confucius' grandson, Tsu-ssu (c.483–c.402 B.C.), but was destined to enlarge upon his master's work. Tsu-ssu explained Confucius' concept of "Jen" as that of "Chung-yung" (mean). He felt that the first step toward it was "Hsiao" (filial piety), which could be achieved through "Chung" (loyalty). Tsu-ssu wrote a book entitled *Chungyung* (The Doctrine of the Mean) and came from the upper part of the Bodhisattva Realm. He had the important role of inheriting the teachings of Confucius and transmitting them to Mencius.

Mencius lived during the Warring States period and is famous for his belief in the original inborn goodness of human nature that is bestowed from heaven. He also believed that every person has four innate feelings—commiseration (compassion, conscience), shame (making us feel ashamed of and hate evil), modesty (which allows us to humble ourselves before others), and justice (the ability to discriminate between right and wrong)—which he claimed proved the innate goodness of humankind. Moreover, he stated that these innate feelings can be further developed into the four moral virtues: commiseration into "Jen" (benevolence), shame into "Yi" (righteousness), modesty into "Li" (propriety), and justice into "Chi" (wisdom). In this way, Mencius explained Confucius' teachings on "Jen" in an analytical and concrete manner.

Later, during the Han period, "Hsin" (fidelity) was added to these four to create what was henceforth to be known as the five cardinal virtues. Unlike the Noble Eightfold Path or Six Paramitas of Buddhism, Mencius' teachings do not deal with the other world; and they are unique in that they deal with propriety, which is something that Shakyamuni Buddha did not teach. Mencius was a Brahma, which means that he came from the highest regions of the Bodhisattva Realm.

At approximately the same time that Mencius died, a philosopher named Hsun-tzu (298–235 B.C.) was born. However, he took the opposite view to that of his predecessor, saying that humans were innately evil and that it was their nature to do wrong. He said that people were essentially selfish, resulting in an unruly scramble that only the fittest could survive and that "Li" (propriety) was necessary to improve on this state. Hsun-tzu was later reincarnated in Europe as Thomas Hobbes (1588–1679), famous for his work *Leviathan*. He is from the Light Realm.

8. The Philosophy of Leisure

The teachings of Confucius and Mencius could be described as a doctrine of effort. It was a positive and constructive philosophy designed to attain human perfection and create an ideal nation. Both Confucius and Mencius were high spirits who came down to Earth with the express object of dealing with human development and the building of the world of the Eternal Buddha or utopia here on Earth.

There was another Great Guiding Spirit of Light, however, whose teachings were of an entirely different type. His name was Lao-tzu and he is famous for being the founder of Taoism. There is some question as to exactly when he lived; some claim that he lived during the Chou period while others say that he was from the Warring States period, which would put him later than Confucius.

In order to settle this dispute, I looked him up in the Akashic Records in the Real World and learned that he was born in 587 and died in 502 B.C.. This would mean that he was Confucius' senior by thirty-five years. They were both active in the same period and Lao-tzu lived to the age of eighty-five.

In his book *Historical Memoirs*, Ssu-ma Ch'ien recounts an episode in which the young Confucius questions Lao-tzu about the Way—this is a true story. At the time, Confucius was a young man of about thirty and full of vigor, while Lao-tzu was already sixty-five years old with the reputation and presence of a great thinker. There was also a great contrast between them in appearance: at nearly two meters (six feet five inches) tall, Confucius was a good-looking, slender young man, while Lao-tzu was a small, thickset man just over one-and-a-half meters (five feet two inches) tall.

When Confucius asked about the Way, Lao-tzu saw straight through the young man's ostentation and replied:

You appear to be a very intelligent man and I can see from your face that you have studied very hard. However, as long as your ambition remains so obvious, you will not be able to succeed. Ambitious men are shunned by those in power, so you must live more simply and naturally, and try to be less pretentious. If you do this, you will become like the great pine tree that has lived for hundreds of years or like the Yellow River that flows majestically down to the sea.

These words had a powerful effect on the young Confucius, but he chose to find another way. He felt that while a life lived the natural way should command respect, humans differ from the rest of nature. Having once been born on this Earth, they have a duty to improve their soul. This was the fundamental idea upon which Confucius built his philosophy and it has a lot in common with the teachings of Shakyamuni, who had lived a little earlier.

It is true that Lao-tzu's philosophy of leisure may not spur everybody to self-improvement. However, looking back over several thousand years of Chinese history, I do not think I am alone in thinking that his "Great Way" of unity with nature could be considered a philosophy of leisure that enables people to enjoy peace of mind.

Lao-tzu used the word "nature" to apply to two things. One was the Earth, which he considered to be "the mother of all things," or "Hsuan p'in" in Chinese. The other was inaction or "Hsuan-te" (unselfishness, innocence, disinterestedness, and unpretentiousness), in other words, avoiding all unnatural acts and living in harmony with nature. Lao-tzu held the view that everyone should return to a life of ease and living at one with nature. This being his philosophy, Lao-tzu's view of an ideal country was that of a "small country, small population." In other words, he wanted a small society, inhabited by people who were pure at heart, a place where force and coercion had been eliminated, where only the gentle, who repaid hatred with virtue, would win the hearts of the people. It is obvious that Lao-tzu based his ideal society on a village that exists in the Real World. It is a fact that in the Tathagata Realm of the eighth dimension where he came from, society comprises gentle people who live in small groups surrounded by a confusion of flowering plants that represent the full wonder of nature. The ultimate difference between Confucius and Lao-tzu can be summed up by saying one was an *educator* of the heavenly realm and the other an *inhabitant* of the heavenly realm.

Lao-tzu's philosophy was passed down to Chuang-tzu (367–279 B.C.) who adapted it to say, "Enjoy the Way." According to Chuan-tzu, "The Way" is something in which all beings are subject to creation, destruction, and change according to the rules of Earth and nature, while it is itself immune from creation, change, and destruction. "The Way" also transcends all restrictions of space and time while itself existing throughout all time and space. Therefore, those who have attained "The Way" can cast off their cleverness, lose their prejudice, and enjoy a life of peace and freedom. This is what Chuang-tzu called "Yu" (idling). Chuang-tzu was a psychic who often visited the heavenly realm through astral travel and, having this experience to enjoy, he thought nothing of worldly values, comparison, or discrimination.

In a past life, Chuang-tzu was born in Greece as Eros, the son of Hermes and Aphrodite. Later, he was born as the great thinker René Descartes (1596–1650), who is sometimes referred to as the father of modern philosophy and who is famous for his book *Discourse on Method*. Then, his brother soul was incarnated in Austria as Franz Kafka (1883–1924), who was famous for such unique books as *Metamorphosis* and *The Trial*. Kafka was apparently also a psychic. Chuang-tzu came from the upper reaches of Tathagata Realm in the eighth dimension (the Sun Realm) and a branch of his spirit was later incarnated as the Japanese Buddhist priest, Saigyo Hoshi, in the twelfth century.

The philosophies of Lao-tzu and Chuang-tzu were further revitalized in the Wei and Chin periods of the third century when they were discussed by the Seven Sages of the Bamboo Grove, a group of wise men who escaped into the forest to avoid persecution. One of the Seven Sages, Yuan Chi (210–263), was against formal etiquette and is famous for welcoming recluses but frowning on worldly people. He has been reincarnated in the present day as the Japanese political and economic critic, Ken'ichi Takemura.

9. The Teaching of Love and Knowledge

I think you will have realized from what I have written so far that Confucianism and Taoism represent the two major streams of Chinese philosophical history, but numerous other philosophers lived and worked during the Ch'un-Ch'iu and Warring States periods, although they never achieved anything like the size or influence of these two great sages.

The first and brightest of these was Mo-tzu (c.480–c.390 B.C.), a philosopher of the Ch'un-Ch'iu period. Like Confucius, Mo-tzu was born in the province of Lu; his family name was Mo and his first name Ti. He became an official of the Sung government, but he is famous for having opposed Confucius' philosophy. There were two main themes to his philosophy: mutual love and pacifism. His doctrine concerning mutual love is very easy to understand and meant, simply, unconditional love. While recognizing that Confucius' "Jen" was also a philosophy of love, Mo-tzu felt that "Jen" contained degrees of love, depending on the relationship of the recipient. He criticized "Jen," calling it "discriminatory love" and arguing for the superiority of indiscriminate love. He said that we should love others as if they were ourselves and that, if we did, there would be no more wars between nations, no more fights between individuals. It is because we love only ourselves, because we do not love others or other countries, that the strong oppress the weak, that majorities exploit the minorities, that the rich trample over the poor, and that the nobility oppress the commoners. He said that we should change our ways to mutual love and work for the mutual profit of all.

This was Mo-tzu's basic teaching on love, and I am sure that there are many of you who will be amazed at its similarity with Jesus Christ's call to "love thy neighbor." However, this is hardly surprising when you consider that it was part of Jesus Christ's spirit that came down through the Tathagata Realm of the eighth dimension to be born as Mo-tzu and preached this gospel as a precursor to his gospel of love. Of course, Mo-tzu's character was different from that of Jesus, but they were both part of the same life form.

Mo-tzu preached pacifism as part of his message of love. At the same time, he praised hard work while criticizing unearned income, luxury and splendor. He even avoided Confucius' ideas on propriety, saying that they represented a type of formalism. His ideas were all based on the belief that humans were all children of God and that the true essence of God was love. Mo-tzu had an unexpectedly practical side to his character, too; he was also famous as a military strategist and armaments production engineer. However, Mo-tzu's basic ideas on the equality of all men and the goodness of other peoples and nations was a little optimistic for the time and did not go down very well with those in power. Later, Emperor Shih Huangti of the Ch'in dynasty issued the Burning of the Books decree, which resulted in the loss of most of Mo-tzu's writings, while the Emperor Han Wu-ti of the Han dynasty ordered that Confucianism should be the national religion. Consequently, the teachings of Mo-tzu, which had been critical of Confucius, went into decline. Despite this, however, the fact that such a philosophy of love existed in China, a country that takes such pride in its eternal mountains and rivers, deserves our greatest admiration.

In complete contrast to Mo-tzu's doctrine of mutual love, we have Hsun-tzu's idea that human nature is basically evil, which I explained in Section 7. This philosophy was to have a strong influence on Han-fei (281–233 B.C.), a legalist and thinker of the late Warring States period. He was also influenced by the work of Shang Yang (397–338 B.C.) and proposed a system of politics based on reward and punishment. He offered his counsel to the king of the Han state, which was one of the seven major territories left at the end of the Warring States period, but it was rejected.

This rejection roused him to write a work entitled *Han-fei-tzu*, in which he described a royalist autocracy based on bureaucracy. Put in simple terms, he said that in order to strengthen the King's power, the whole population should be subjugated and laws created to achieve this. He realized the inherent danger of this, however, and said that although these laws would have the power to control the people, measures would be needed to control those who wielded them.

Han-fei was later reincarnated in Renaissance Italy as Niccolo Machiavelli (1469–1527), as whom he again concerned himself with political thought, writing *The Prince* and developing his own school of thought that was later to become known as Machiavellianism. He was criticized for his idea that in politics the end justifies the means, but at the time Italy was beset by foes both at home and abroad and his views were in fact the result of cool, objective thought. He is said to be the forerunner of modern political science.

Machiavelli had a subconscious memory of his previous life as Han-fei when he was sent to the Ch'in court as a messenger and earned the envy of Li-ssu (282–208 B.C.), who poisoned him. Again, he held an important post in the republican government of Florence, but lost it with the restoration of the Medici regime. As a result of these experiences, he tended to be rather suspicious of others. He is now studying politics in the Light Realm of the sixth dimension.

10. The Light of Confucianism Remains Bright

More than two thousand years have passed since the age of "One Hundred Schools." During most of this time, Confucianism has been studied as a scholastic subject necessary in order to advance in the world rather than for its religious significance. Confucius comes from the ninth dimension, the same as Shakyamuni Buddha or Jesus, but strangely enough, Confucianism has very little religious flavor.

This very fact gives us some idea of the depth of Confucius' intellect. Whereas Christianity and Buddhism have in many respects been isolated from secular power, Confucianism has always remained at the very center of politics. It was indeed an ingenious way of spreading the word. Instead of just preaching of heaven and hell, leading people blindly into fanaticism, Confucianism spoke of the way to human perfection, and was an important method of directing people along the road to improvement. It is a fact that Confucius was one of the greatest educators the world has ever known, with a deep understanding of essential human nature. I believe that it is important for religion in the future to combine faith, intellect and reason, and, in this sense, I think I would be right in saying that there is a need for a new Confucian-like philosophy.

During the Northern Sung dynasty, about one thousand five hundred years after Confucius lived, there appeared a Confucian scholar named Chou Tun-i (1017–1073). He was to go on to found Neo-Confucianism and was an inhabitant of the upper Light Realm. His teachings were carried on by

Chu Hsi (1130–1200), who brought them to completion. Chu Hsi was a scholar of the Southern Sung dynasty and is most famous for his books *Reflections on Things at Hand*, *Notes on the Collection of the Four Books*, and *Items for a Comprehensive Mirror for Aid in Government*. So influential was he to be that later a new branch of Confucianism was named after him. As I mention in Chapter Two, Section 3, he was from the Brahma Realm and was once incarnated in Rome where he lived his life as the philosopher Cicero.

To give a brief summary of Chu Hsi's philosophy, it focused on "Li," which is a metaphysical "Way" and the source of material objects, and on "Ch'i," which is a physical substance that provides the raw material of objects. "Li" is what brings this world into existence, but it is not something that exists in isolation either within or without the world; "Li" is all one and exists undivided in everything. It is like the moon in that we see numerous images of it reflected in lakes and ponds but there is only one. This theory of Chu Hsi's is very reminiscent of the philosophy propounded by Plato and this is probably due to the fact that Chu Hsi had a vestigial memory of having heard Plato's theory during his existence as Cicero.

There was another great scholar of the Southern Sung dynasty, named Lu Hsiang-shan, whose views put him in direct opposition to Chu Hsi. Whereas Chu Hsi taught a dualistic doctrine of the metaphysical "Li" and the physical "Chi," Lu Hsiang-shan held a monistic view, saying that everything in the universe existed in a person's mind, and, at the same time, the mind itself existed in the universe. Whereas Chu Hsi considered the mind to hold the balance of the yin and yang (the positive and passive elements of the universe), therefore making the mind a physical object, Lu Hsiang-shan thought it metaphysical. For this reason, he could be described as taking a spiritualistic position. To put it more simply, he felt that every possible activity in the universe was one reflected in our minds and that the universe only exists because we exist, while we only exist because the universe exists.

This philosophy appears to be very similar to the monistic thought of Plotinus, an ancient Roman philosopher who claimed that all matter emanated from the one and only substance. The reason for this similarity is that Lu Hsiang-shan had received guidance from Plotinus in the Real World. As I stated in Section 5 of this chapter, Lu Hsiang-shan was the reincarnation of Vasubandhu who brought Mahayana Buddhism to its peak in India. He was a spirit from the upper part of the Bodhisattva Realm.

Lu Hsiang-shan's theory was later inherited by Wang Yang-ming (1472–1529) during the Ming dynasty. Wang Yang-ming declared that the mind was "Li" and that no objects or "Li" existed outside the mind. For instance, he said that there is no such thing as the "Li" of filial piety or loyalty somewhere outside the mind; instead, you should fully manifest the pure, heavenly mind, which is "Li" itself.

While fully manifesting this pure state, if you serve your parents, you are practicing the "Li" of filial piety, and if you serve your master, you are practicing the "Li" of loyalty. According to Wang Yang-ming, a flower blooming among the rocks deep in the mountains is in a state of tranquility, and even this exists within the human mind, too. This spiritualistic philosophy may seem a little difficult to understand, but if it is looked at from the point of view of Buddhist enlightenment, that is to say "experience of the cosmic consciousness," it becomes clear. If the mind is expanded, it becomes infinite; but if it is contracted, it becomes a single point.

Wang Yang-ming also preached that "Knowledge and action are one." This means, for instance, that if you truly knew that you should look after your parents, you would do so without thinking. In other words, there is no difference between thinking and doing. Wang Yang-ming's true intention was to teach the relationship between the thought and action. He was originally from the Tathagata Realm of the eighth dimension and his work was comparable to that of Luther and Calvin in Christianity.

Chapter Four
The Land of the Rising Sun

1. The Gathering of the Gods

In this chapter I would like to look at the high spirits who came down to Japan to carry out plans to Buddha's intent. As a result of this investigation, you will see that Japan can be called "the land of the gods."

The history of the actual Japanese archipelago itself is very old, the islands being formed in their present shape approximately thirty thousand years ago. The culture of the people who lived there underwent a sudden change about fifteen thousand years ago with the arrival of several hundred refugees from the continent of Mu who had managed to escape the destruction of their homeland. They came by sea and settled on one of the four main islands of Japan that is now known as Kyushu (one of the four main islands of Japan, south-west of the main island). They brought with them a knowledge of modern science that made them look like gods in the eyes of the native tribes;

and it was the oral tradition of these events that was to form the basis of Japanese mythology.

The culture of present-day Japan was founded by the high spirits who came down to Earth approximately two thousand eight hundred years ago. In approximately 830 B.C., Ame-no-Minakanushi-no-Mikoto (God Ruling the Center of Heaven) was born on the Takachiho-no-Mine mountain in Kyushu. He was a Tathagata from the very highest area of the eighth dimension who was incarnated in human form with the express purpose of creating the Japanese nation. This was two hundred years before the birth of Shakyamuni, three hundred years before Confucius, and more than three hundred years before Socrates.

Ame-no-Minakanushi-no-Mikoto is often called Ame-no-Minakanushi-no-Kami and described as being a god; in fact, many even consider him to be the cosmic or primordial god. However, human history extends back four hundred million years, well beyond the ken of historians, so a person can hardly be described as a primordial god just because he lived three thousand years ago. Ame-no-Minakanushi-no-Mikoto was a high spirit who worked hard to create the base for modern Japan. What are usually referred to as "kami" (gods in Japanese) were really outstanding human beings with strong personal charisma.

Ame-no-Minakanushi-no-Mikoto was both a powerful politician and a man of religion who built a broad power base in southern Kyushu, based around what is now Miyazaki Prefecture. Of course, there had been many kings in the land before him, but he was the first to suggest that the person who can transmit the words of god should be the one to rule the country. In this sense, he could be said to be the forerunner of the present imperial family, which has long practiced a form of politics based on religion.

Ame-no-Minakanushi-no-Mikoto was a powerful psychic and was renowned for the fact that whatever he said was guaranteed to come true. People were struck with awe at his apparent infallibility. For instance, if he were to announce that one of the neighboring countries would sue for peace on a certain date, he would be correct. If he said that he would build a huge castle within three months, both material and labor would materialize from here and there across the realm and everything would go as he promised. He was infallible in everything he did. On top of this, he could read people's minds so it was impossible for evil men to find a post in his court and this permitted him to base the politics of his nation on virtue. His philosophy could be described as being a "Monism of Light," and he summed it up in the words "The truth lies only in goodness, the truth lies only in light." So resolute was he in this belief, that he was actually successful in creating a land of light through the creative power of words. His people were so proud of him that he was worshipped as a kind of primordial god for centuries.

The nation that Ame-no-Minakanushi-no-Mikoto created in southern Kyushu was known as Takachiho and he was succeeded to the throne by a man named Taka-Mi-

Musuhi-no-Mikoto (Kami). The throne was not passed down on a hereditary basis; rather, Ame-no-Minakanushi-no-Mikoto chose to abdicate in favor of his successor. Taka-Mi-Musuhi-no-Mikoto was a noble who was also both a powerful mystic and a virtuous man. He was a particularly gifted clairvoyant and knew the plans of all the countries hostile to his own, making him invincible in battle.

The third king of this nation was a man called Kamu-Musuhi-no-Kami who was particularly gifted in talking to the spirits. He was instructed in the running of the country by Ame-no-Minakanushi-no-Mikoto, who had already returned to the heavenly realm by this time. All three of the kings of Takachiho were from the Tathagata Realm of the eighth dimension and their works heightened the standing of the Shinto religion.

2. The Appearance of a Beautiful Goddess

In approximately 765 B.C. a man named Izanagi-no-Mikoto was born in what is now Oita Prefecture in Kyushu. When he was twenty-four years old, he met Izanami-no-Mikoto and the two of them married. Soon afterwards, a girl was born who was later to be known as Amaterasu-O-Mikami (the Sun Goddess). Two years after that, a son was born who was named Susanoo-no-Mikoto. Amaterasu-O-Mikami, having a gentle disposition, took after her mother, whereas her brother was a very fierce man.

Amaterasu-O-Mikami is often referred to as the supreme or principal deity in the Shinto religion of Japan and this is because she was the first empress, that is to say, the first queen of Takachiho. She was the fifth monarch in the line that began with Ame-no-Minakanushi-no-Mikoto. The reason why it was decided that she should become monarch was that Ame-no-Minakanushi-no-Mikoto had sent a message from the Tathagata Realm of the eighth dimension saying, "In order that our land become a beautiful and lovely one, it is time that it be ruled by a woman. Look for a virtuous man by the name of Izanagi-no-Mikoto who lives in our land and offer the throne to his daughter. She is to be the next ruler." In this way, during the age of gods, rulers were selected through divine messages from heaven. This is not to say that they were necessarily permitted to rule forever; if a ruler had evil or greedy thoughts, a message would come demanding that he or she be replaced. In this period there were a large number of people living on the Earth who could communicate with heaven and they were very highly respected by the rest of the populace. It was common for the most talented of these to become leader and run the nation according to the messages they received from heaven. This form of government would be called theocracy.

The messages from the high spirits were quite precise and allowed no room for argument, which resulted in an orderly form of government. In comparison, politicians today are selected on the basis of personal fame; it is the rule of the majority and, as a result, government seems to be in disorder. We seem to be led by people who are blind to the Truth, whose eyes have been dazzled by their lust for power, and modern politicians resemble a mob more than anything else. We can only hope that it will not be long before we see a return to clean politics, led by virtuous men. Amaterasu-O-Mikami was not a member of the royal family; she was merely the daughter of the leader of one of the many clans. But she was accepted as ruler because it had been so commanded from heaven. She was a refined, gentle-mannered woman, but she had about her a godlike dignity that aroused awe in all those who met her. She reigned for about twenty years and, during that period, the national prestige of the country was enhanced and an endless stream of people visited her court to pay tribute.

As I mentioned earlier, Amaterasu-O-Mikami's brother was, in contrast, a fierce warrior. He did not agree with his sister's political opinions and was forever causing her trouble. Amaterasu-O-Mikami aimed to rule her nation in a fair and honest way, and by so doing win the allegiance of the surrounding countries. But Susanoo-no-Mikoto thought very little of this policy. He had several hundred warriors at his command and led them personally into battle against the other nations of Kyushu and western Honshu.

Amaterasu-O-Mikami was active in Japan approximately one hundred years before Shakyamuni appeared in India. Although the true story of her life is veiled in myth, it was not such a long time ago in terms of the history of the Real World and quite a number of details of her reign are readily available. For instance, in the third year of her reign,

Susanoo-no-Mikoto led one thousand warriors on an expedition to subjugate the state of Izumo. At that time, Izumo was ruled by powerful clans, but rather than fight the army that had been brought up against them, the clans sued for peace, the only condition being that Susanoo-no-Mikoto rid them of an eight-headed serpent that lived in the upper reaches of the Hino river. If he succeeded in this, they would give him Princess Kushinada as a token of the new peace between them.

I would like to say a word about this monster, which is known in Japanese mythology as Yamata-no-Orochi. Although they are very rare now, at this time in history a large number of giant reptiles still existed in Japan. According to legend, Yamata-no-Orochi was as large as a mountain, had eight heads and eight tails and trees grew out of the scales of his body. I will now, however, focus my spiritual eye on two thousand six hundred years ago to see what actually happened.

I can see that it is true; there is indeed a gigantic snake living in the upper waters of the Hino river. It had caused a panic by eating some of the local people and, as a result, it was decided to sacrifice a girl to it every year, placing her inside a basket and leaving it outside the entrance to its lair. I can see the villagers placing the basket on the ground then scattering like scared rabbits. Looking inside the cave, I see a giant serpent coiled on the ground. It looks like a cross between a python and a boa constrictor, thirteen meters (forty-two feet) long and with a girth of about one meter (three feet). It does not have eight heads and eight tails as legend would have us believe, but it does have three heads and three tails. I presume that three snakes must have been born together like some kind of Siamese triplets. It is eerie to see its six eyes gleaming in the dark.

Looking at the spiritual body of the monster, I realize that it is not that of a serpent. It would appear that some hermit with great spiritual power has trapped several evil spirits inside its body. I can see the bodies of its past victims lying in the stomach, including that of a warrior who came to kill it, and his sword shines brightly within its body.

Susanoo-no-Mikoto obviously had psychic powers; I see him building an altar in front of Yamata-no-Orochi's lair that he uses to pray to Hachidai-Ryu-O (king of the eight great dragons) for help. Hachidai-Ryu-O binds the evil spirits, allowing Susanoo-no-Mikoto to kill the giant serpent.

The sword that he finds inside the monster's stomach he names Ame-no-Murakumo and takes it back to present to his sister. At around this time Amaterasu-O-Mikami enters a cave and remains there for eighty days, praying that her brother's violent nature be subdued. When she came out again, they made peace with each other, but later he crossed the sea to Korea on a military expedition, leaving her no option but to banish him from Takachiho.

3. The Himiko Period

The fact that a spiritually advanced woman like Amaterasu-O-Mikami became the first queen of the country was to have a lasting influence over the people of Japan. In particular, her feminine qualities of generosity, delicacy, tranquility, elegance, and beauty came to be referred to as Yamato Gogoro, which can be translated as "the spirit of Japan." The inhabitants of the Goddess Realm are considered to be the equals of the male Tathagata, included among them are: Aphrodite and Athena of the Greek gods; Amaterasu-O-Mikami and Toyotama-Hime from Japan; Manjushri, Maitreya and Queen Maya from the Buddhist deities; and the Virgin Mary, Florence Nightingale, and Helen Keller from Christian circles.

Among the goddesses in the group at a level slightly below these, we find Himiko. She was born in Kyushu in about 200 A.D., a time when Jesus and his disciples were all long dead and the fledgling Church was just beginning to prosper. By this time, the power of Amaterasu-O-Mikami's Takachiho had declined until it had become a minor state and the main power in Kyushu was centered along the Ariake Sea coast, commanding a good view of Mt. Aso. This nation was called Yamataikoku by the Chinese who visited it, but in Japan it was known as Yamato and controlled over thirty states in Kyushu. It was later to develop into the Yamato imperial court and hold sway over the whole of Japan.

The name "Himiko" was the Chinese rendition of the Japanese "Himuka," which means "looking towards the sun." Himiko was also a gifted psychic and was guided from heaven by Amaterasu-O-Mikami in both religious and state affairs. This meant that the principle god of the Yamato nation was Amaterasu-O-Mikami, who had herself ruled in Kyushu seven or eight hundred years earlier.

Himiko's politics had three main characteristics. First, she would converse with the spirit world once a week to make the necessary political decisions. Second, she involved a large number of women in politics, and third, she initiated the custom of holding a festival every spring and autumn.

In those days, lineage was considered very important and this resulted in many consanguineous marriages within powerful families. Himiko was no exception to this; her husband was in fact her younger brother. From this blood-line was to come the Emperor Keikou whose son was Yamato-Takeru-no-Mikoto and whose wife was Oto-Tachibana-Hime. This was at around the end of the third century and the beginning of the fourth. It was at this time that the court expanded eastwards from Kyushu up to Nara where a new capital was built.

Recently, there has been some doubt among scholars as to the actual existence of Emperor Jimmu, the first of the line of the present imperial family and the man who is acclaimed as being the hero who led the move to the east. It seems that the stories of his life were based on the exploits of Susanoo-no-Mikoto and Yamato-Takeru-no-Mikoto.

Yamato-Takeru-no-Mikoto is from the Tathagata Realm and is one of the prime nation-builders among the high spirits. In a previous incarnation he had been Han Hsin (third to second century B.C.), and was responsible for the creation of the Han dynasty in China. He was born again in Japan in the nineteenth century as Aritomo Yamagata (1838–1922), General of the Army, in which form he was responsible for making Japan into a major military power.

4. The Politics of Prince Shotoku

About three hundred and fifty years after Himiko, the Yamato court had become settled in the area around Nara and was becoming increasingly powerful. From 513 A.D., numerous scholars of the Chinese classics were sent to Japan from Pekjae, a state in Korea, an act that resulted in the spread of Confucianism in Japan. In 538 A.D., King Song-myong Wang of Pekjae officially presented Japan with various Buddhist scriptures and sutras. Buddhist teachings had already reached Japan about one hundred years earlier through private commerce and so the time was ripe for the introduction of Buddhist scriptures. The importation of foreign civilization was at its peak during the sixth century. In this respect it resembles the late nineteenth century, when Western ideas swept the country.

It was against this background that the second son of Emperor Yomei, the man who was later to become famous as Shotoku Taishi or Prince Shotoku (574–622), was born. He acted as regent for his aunt, Empress Suiko, and during this time he overhauled the government's domestic and external policies, laying the foundation for the centralized state. In 603 A.D., he established a system of twelve grades for courtiers, each grade represented by a different colored hat. This system cut across the traditional system of hereditary rank and offered opportunities for a wider range of people to rise in public office. While the old system of rank was based entirely on family nobility, the new one was based on character strengths. This idea still exists in today's civil service, illustrating that it still retains its novelty even after more than one thousand years.

The twelve cap-ranks were very much influenced by Confucianism and were named as follows: virtue, benevolence, propriety, faith, justice, and knowledge, each of these six being divided into "greater" and "lesser" to produce the twelve. Prince Shotoku's idea in producing these ranks was to do away with the system of inherited office and to place rank according not so much to ability, but character. In other words, Prince Shotoku wanted to recreate the hierarchy of the Real World upon Earth.

His second policy move was to draw up a seventeen-article constitution that shows the influences of Confucianism, Buddhism, and Chinese Legalism. The object of the constitution was the establishment of Confucian order, a declaration of Buddhist Truth and the establishment of political principles. Prince Shotoku was a brilliant man and in a remarkably short time had been able to absorb the philosophies of the Buddhists, the Confucians, the Legalists, and the Taoists, and master them all.

The first article is particularly important and reads, "Harmony is to be treasured and an absence of disagreement honored." This spirit so imbued the Japanese character that it remains a part of national policy to this very day, and is also to be found in contemporary business circles. Prince Shotoku's aim was to build a utopia in the minds of each individual that would lead to the whole nation becoming a land of Buddha.

Article ten says, "Refrain from wrath and cast off angry thoughts. Do not become resentful when others differ from you, as everyone has a mind and every mind has its own leanings. Their right is our wrong and our right is their wrong. We are not all infallible sages neither are we all unequivocally fools. We are all just ordinary people. Although others may give way to anger, we should consider our own faults. Even if you alone are in the right, try and follow the majority and act like them." This reflects the idea that we are all children of Buddha and therefore all one.

Article fourteen states, "Ministers and subjects, do not envy. If we envy others, they in turn will envy us. The evils of envy know no limit.... If we do not find wise men and sages, how will the country be governed?" Here again, the teachings of the mind and the way to the ideal state are in harmony with each other. In other words, Prince Shotoku was fully aware of the truth that "the state of mind of those who come in contact with us is a mirror of our own."

In article seventeen he says, "Decisions on important matters should not be made by one person alone. They should be discussed by many." This is the basic principle of democracy and, considering that this constitution was drawn up in 604, it is easy to see that Prince Shotoku was born more than a thousand years before his time, or, rather, that the Truth remains never changing.

However, if we remember that Prince Shotoku was in fact a reincarnation of the Greek statesman Solon, as I related in Chapter Two, we realize that political truth is not very liable to change. The entire seventeen-article constitution reflects his intention to govern through enlightenment, and his high moral standing becomes obvious through the form of government he inspired. It represents a harmony of democracy and government by virtue. Personally, I see in it a fusion of the democracy of the polis or city-states of ancient Greece and of Plato's philosophy, government by a philosopher-king.

In 607, Prince Shotoku sent Ono-no-Imoko as an envoy to the Sui court in China to open diplomatic relations and learn from the more advanced continental culture. Here again, we see the unique Japanese trait of importing foreign culture and then adapting it until it becomes something uniquely Japanese.

One of Prince Shotoku's greatest achievements was the role he played in spreading Buddhism. In particular, he wrote a book entitled *A Treatise on Three Sutras*, and founded several temples, most importantly Horyu-ji Temple in Nara and Shiten'no-ji Temple in Osaka. At his death, he left these last words for his wife, Tachibana-no-Iratsume, "The world is false, Buddha alone is real," and to his son, Tamura-no-Miko, he said, "Worldly treasure is easily destroyed and should not be kept for long but the Dharma of the Three Jewels—the Buddha, the Dharma, and the Sangha—is eternal and should be passed on for ever." From this, it can be seen that Shotoku Taishi was a great Tathagata who laid the framework for the country of Japan.

5. Saicho and the Tendai Sect

Following the death of Prince Shotoku began the period known in Japanese history as Nara period (710–784) when Buddhism was practiced as a state religion. During this period, Buddhism became rather scholarly, dividing into six sects: Sanron, Hosso, Jojitsu, Kusha, Kegon and Ritsu, each devoting themselves to the study of the sutras. This period was notable for the casting of the huge bronze image of Buddha at Todai-ji Temple in the capital city Nara, and the rise of Buddhism as the basic philosophy to pacify and defend the country. Later, in 794, the Emperor Kanmu moved the capital to Heian (as Kyoto was then called), marking the beginning of the Heian period (794–1192). Two spirits were incarnated on Earth during the Heian period who represent the religious movements of the time.

First there was Saicho (767–822), who was closely followed by Kukai (774–835). Saicho is famous for founding the Tendai sect in Japan, and is often referred to by the honorific name Dengyo Daishi, which means "the master who transmitted the teaching." He was born in the province of Omi (present-day Shiga Prefecture). At the age of fourteen he went to study under a local priest named

Gyohyo. In 785 he left his formal training and went to live in a small grass-roofed hut on Mt. Hiei where he studied the scriptures in solitude. Eventually he arrived at the "One Vehicle" philosophy, which stated that anyone could become a Buddha. Deciding to form a new branch of Buddhism in Japan, he traveled to China in 804 to further his studies. This was the same period that Kukai was studying in China, but Saicho returned in 805, after only one year, founding the Tendai-Hokke sect in 806 and holding heated debates with the powerful established sects in Nara. Most famous of these debates was one with Tokuitsu of the Hosso sect on the expediency and truth concerning the "One Vehicle" and "Three Vehicles" philosophies. The Hosso sect believed that there were three different stages of spirituality that could be achieved by the seeker of the Truth, hence the name "three vehicles," whereas Saicho was an exponent of the "one vehicle" philosophy that claimed that anybody could become a Buddha. Saicho became the target of fierce opposition from the accepted Nara sects, who held a monopoly on the ordination of priests, and he devoted his life to creating an independent Mahayana ordination for the Tendai sect. He wrote several works, the most famous being *Manifesting the Precepts* and *The Origin of the Manifestation of Precepts*.

If we look at the life of this famous priest from the point of view of the Real World, we see that he was a high spirit from the Bodhisattva Realm whose mission on Earth was to travel to China and bring the Tendai faith back to Japan. To this end, he received spiritual instruction from the founder of this sect, Master T'ien-t'ai himself. Unfortunately, however, from about the time of his debates with Tokuitsu of the Hosso sect, Saicho became overcome by feelings of aggression, the lust for fame and pride. While the Tendai "One Vehicle" philosophy, which states that anyone can become a Buddha, is correct in that we are all children of Buddha and all share equal possibilities and hope, Saicho failed to realize that there are different levels of enlightenment that can be achieved by those searching for the Truth. It is a fact that the Real World is generally divided into six levels, from the fourth to the ninth dimension, according to the inhabitants' level of enlightenment. Therefore, although we are all children of Buddha, we all belong to different levels according to the extent that we have manifested our divine nature, or Buddha nature. In this respect, Tokuitsu's belief in three levels of enlightenment was much closer to the Truth.

To put it simply, Saicho was overcome by impatience and resorted to political trickery in an attempt to establish his particular variety of Buddhism. His impatience was only increased by the jealousy he felt of the young genius, Kukai, who by then had returned from China. The Truth can be divided into two halves, the wisdom of equality and the wisdom of discrimination, but Saicho learned only the wisdom of equality and believed that this was all there was and started to attack the established Nara-based sects fiercely. This idea proved to be a serious flaw in his teaching [Tendai Hongaku Philosophy, Author's Note 2, p. 217]. In addition to this, he was filled with arrogance, pride and jealousy, and for nearly 1,200 years since his death in 822 he has been repenting of his acts when on Earth. He was basically a pure-hearted, strict man and he has been unable to forgive himself for the dark clouds that have hung over Mt. Hiei as a result of his sect's involvement in political struggles, or for the number of priests who have lost their way as a result of the mistakes contained in his teachings that have spread so widely.

6. Kukai and Esoteric Buddhism

Kukai, also known as Kobo Daishi, (774–835) was a contemporary of Saicho, being born only seven years after him. He was born into the Saeki clan in the Sanuki province (present-day Kagawa Prefecture), and at the age of fifteen was sent to a national college in Nara where he was soon recognized as a genius. However, he soon became disenchanted with the idea of an official career and at the age of twenty left to travel around the country.

He did not take up Buddhism for worldly fame; rather, he wanted to share the experience that Shakyamuni had undergone in achieving enlightenment. Trying to emulate Shakyamuni in every way, Kukai renounced a secular life and began traveling around the mountains and fields of Shikoku. He adopted the practice of meditating under a waterfall in the southern part of Tokushima, then moved through the mountains to Tosa (present-day Kochi Prefecture). Later, at Mt. Otaki in Awa (present-day Tokushima Prefecture), he met a hermit who offered him some valuable advice:

You will not find your way through meditating under a waterfall; you need to go somewhere where you can see the sky and the sea. You should follow the coast southwards as far as Hiwasa village, then, taking a hatchet, you should cut a path through the woods. If you are not bitten by a poisonous snake en route, you should arrive at Murotozaki, where the demons are said to appear, within two days.

This hermit was a psychic who had the power to read minds. At this time Kukai was eager to master a supernatural power called Kokuzo-Gumonji-Ho (a method of enhancing the abilities to understand and memorize all the Buddhist scriptures) but, as the hermit said, this was not something that he could achieve through meditating under waterfalls. Kukai headed for the Murotozaki (Muroto Cape) as the hermit suggested, and when he arrived at the very tip of the cape, now called Hotsumisaki, he found a cave that would be ideal for his purposes. Shakyamuni had achieved enlightenment after meditating in the state of the Middle Way under the Bodhi tree for seven days, and Kukai aimed to emulate this.

Using my second sight I can see a cave; the entrance is two and a half meters (eight feet) in diameter and it is about twenty meters (sixty-five feet) in depth. It would appear to have been carved out of the cliffs by the waves of the Pacific. Kukai sat and meditated here for approximately twenty days, eating roasted rice he had carried with him and roots that he found in the surrounding mountains. The miracle occurred at dawn of the fifteenth day.

Kukai was meditating when his body started to vibrate backwards and forwards then grow in size. He emerged from the cave and looked down on the wild waters below him. Next, before he realized what was happening, the morning star appeared and flew straight into the mouth of his enormous body. At that moment, he underwent a miraculous experience and became one with the universe. He was twenty years and seven months old.

He knew he would never forget the view he had been granted of the sky and the sea while he was in his gigantic form and that was when he first began to call himself Kukai, which means "sky and sea." As a result of this experience, he gained the powers of both clairvoyance and clairaudience and began to communicate with the spirits of the Real World. His guiding spirits at this time were Shakyamuni Buddha, who appeared in the form of Mahavairocana (Dainichi Tathagata), and Amoghavajra (Fuku Sanzo). Later, acting on the directions of Amoghavajra, Kukai traveled to China in 804 and studied under the priest Hui-kuo (746–805) at Ch'ang-an. Shortly before Hui-Kuo died, he named Kukai as his successor.

Kukai returned to Japan in 806 and set about founding the Shingon (True Word) sect of esoteric Buddhism while looking rather coldly at Saicho who was very active in the capital. Ten years later, in 816, he opened Kongobu-ji Temple on Mt. Koya and this marked the official beginning of the Shingon sect in Japan. Later still, in 823, To-ji temple in Kyoto was placed at the disposal of the Shingon sect and this led to the increased popularity of this form of esoteric Buddhism. Kukai considered *exoteric* Buddhism like that practiced by Saicho's Tendai sect to be simply a way of educating the living. In Kukai's view, the true purpose of religious self-discipline is to attain enlightenment that will enable spiritual salvation, and *esoteric* Buddhism was the only teaching that fulfilled this purpose. Today, esoteric Buddhism is often regarded as a kind of shamanism, but its original aim was to return to Buddhism in its original form and to recapture the spirit that existed when Shakyamuni first attained enlightenment.

Kukai's greatness lies in the fact that while he preached that Buddhahood could be attained in this existence, he never lost his desire to help the masses, something that the Theravada Buddhists were not interested in. This fact is evident from his deeds, such as the creation of the Manno-ike reservoir in Sanuki or the Shugei-Shuchi-in school he founded in Kyoto in 828 to teach Buddhism and Confucianism to the students from common families. Kukai is presently studying the Law in the Tathagata Realm of the eighth dimension and the main theme of his studies is "the characteristics of willpower." His theory is that a person's happiness or misery depends on the nature of that person's will, so he is studying the ways to control it. He is also writing a book on the Truth that goes far beyond *The Treatise on the Ten Stages of the Development of the Mind*, which he wrote while he was alive. It can be assumed that it was their relative enthusiasm for the study of the Law that dictated the positions in which Kukai and Saicho now find themselves.

However, if we were to look for a flaw in Kukai's teaching, it would have to be the idea that full enlightenment is attainable in this existence. In the only book that is left to us by Tokuitsu, *Questions on the Doctrine of Shingon Sect*, he writes that Shingon esoteric Buddhism is lacking in "self-discipline" and "compassion." While criticizing the Shingon sect from his own position within the Hosso sect, Tokuitsu questions whether enlightenment in this existence could really be possible. It is true that the idea of enlightenment in this existence has a lot in common with Hongaku philosophy and there is some danger that it might lead to a desire for instantaneous enlightenment.

One of the members of the Shingon sect who was to fall into this trap was Kakuban (1095–1143). He attempted to combine the Shingon esoteric practices with the faith of the Jodo (Pure Land) sect that was very popular at that time. To this end, he promoted a radical form of esoteric Nembutsu (chanting), claiming that all one needed to do to achieve enlightenment in this existence was to chant the mantras. At one point he had the support of the ex-Emperor Toba and his sect grew rapidly, but later he was forcibly driven out by the priests at Kongobu-ji temple and escaped to Negoro in Wakayama Prefecture where he met a bitter death. He is often praised by esoteric Buddhists as being the father of the Neo Shingon sect, but the fact is that after his death he fell to hell, where he continues his activities as the devil. He is responsible for two heretical esoteric new religious movements that are popular today, the Shin'nyo-en and the Agon-shu.

The idea of enlightenment in this existence, as preached by Kukai, is subject largely to the abilities of the individual seeker of the Truth. This can be seen by the fact that whereas his ten disciples (Jichie, Shinzei, Shinga, Taihan, Chisen, Shin'nyo, Do-o, Enmyo, Gorin, and Chuen) were all very accomplished, those who came later could not reach the same heights.

However, Kukai's theory of enlightenment in this existence differs from the simplistic Tendai Hongaku philosophy for the following reason: In his book *Mystic Mandara of Treatise on the Ten Stages of the Development of the Mind*, Kukai presented his philosophy of "ju-jushin." [Author's Note 3, p. 218] This stated that a person's state of mind is divided into ten stages and that a different level of teaching is required for each stage. This work ranks with T'ien-t'ai Chih-i's philosophy of "five periods and eight teachings" [Author's Note 4, p. 219] or *Discourse on Mahayana Meditation and Contemplation*. In comparison with the degraded Tendai Hongaku philosophy, which preached that salvation could be achieved through the invocation and chanting of a phrase of the sutras, Kukai's work demonstrates that he was a superior religious thinker.

7. The Popularity of the Pure Land Sect

There was one more school of thought in Buddhism that was prevalent at around this time and that was the Jodo (Pure Land) sect. This sect believed that by begging for help from the Amitabha Buddha through the single-minded chanting of Amitabha's name, one would be reborn in Amitabha's Western Paradise, which is known as the Pure Land, and enjoy everlasting happiness. I am sure that many of you will notice that this bears a resemblance to Christianity. However, this is hardly surprising. El Cantare, who led the Mahayana movement of Buddhism from High Divine Realm, commissioned Jesus Christ to take a leading role in the salvation movement on Earth, and the disciples of Jesus were later reincarnated as Buddhist monks and priests to develop the philosophy of the Pure Land sect.

In his interpretation of Vasubandhu's *Treatise on the Pure Land*, which he entitled *An Annotated Treatise on the Pure Land*, the Chinese monk T'an-luan (476-542) stated that the way to the Truth was divided into two; the Easy Way of Practice and the Hard Way of Practice. The Easy way of Practice employs the help of an outside power, therefore making it the ideal vehicle for the common man to find salvation.

Later, Tao-cho (562–645), in his book *Collection of Passages on Birth in the Pure Land*, divided Buddhism into the Holy Way Gate (Self Power Way) and the Pure Land Gate (Other Power Way) and said that in the period of decadent Dharma (the Latter Day of the Law), the best way to attain rebirth in the Pure Land was to call upon the help of the Amitabha Buddha. This philosophy was then handed down to Shan-tao (613–681) in the early Tang dynasty, who said that to embrace and believe in Amitabha's original vow to save humankind, and the chanting of the words "Namu Amida Butsu" (taking refuge in Amitabha Buddha), would be a proper way of self-discipline. In this way, the Pure Land sect was perfected in China.

As the concept of "the period of decadent Dharma" became widespread in Japan during the late twelfth century, the belief in the Pure Land gained popularity. A famous priest named Genshin (942–1017) had a great influence on the founding of the Pure Land sects. He was born in Yamato province (Nara Prefecture) and at the age of thirteen left home to study at Enryaku-ji Temple on Mt. Hiei under the priest Ryogen before preaching salvation through the chanting of the name of Amitabha Buddha.

Genshin was John the Baptist in an earlier incarnation, and in this form he had baptized Jesus Christ who was then thirty years old. Later, he was born again in Sweden as Emanuel Swedenborg (1688–1772), a famous scientist, theosophist and mystic who wrote prolifically on his travels to the spirit world. In his life as Genshin, too, he was very adept at astral travel in the spirit world and repeatedly left his body to visit the realms of heaven and hell. It was these experiences that permitted him to write his vivid descriptions of heaven, hell and the six paths, the famous part in his *Essentials of Pure Land Rebirth*, a collection of excerpts of various sutras.

At the core of Genshin's philosophy was the belief that there existed three stages to salvation. First and foremost there was Rikan (contemplation)—to meditate on the Truth of the Tendai creed. For those who could not attain this there was Jikan (meditation)—contemplation on the image of Buddha. Finally, for the wicked masses, he recommended Shomyonembutsu (invocation)—the chanting of the name of Amitabha Buddha, although he considered this to be only a temporary expedient. This temporary measure was adopted by Ryonin (1072–1132) and then passed on to the next period in Japanese history. Genshin was a spirit from the Tathagata Realm.

In this way the flow of the Pure-Land belief trickled down through the years until it was adopted by Honen (1133–1212) and became a roaring torrent. Honen was born to a local lord in Mimasaka province (Okayama Prefecture), but joined the priesthood at the age of nine upon the death of his father. He finally entered Enryaku-ji Temple on Mt. Hiei at the age of fifteen, where he became a student of Eiku at Kurodani. At the age of forty three, he developed the creed of the exclusive chanting of Amitabha's name, basing his philosophy on *Notes on the Meditation of Sutras* by the Chinese monk Shan-tao and on Genshin's *Essentials of*

Pure Land Rebirth. Soon after this Honen moved to Yoshimizu in Higashiyama, Kyoto, where he concentrated on spreading this new form of worship, finding many converts among both nobles and commoners and becoming very famous. However, he was met by fierce opposition from the established Buddhist sects in Nara and Mt. Hiei and was eventually banished to Sanuki province (Kagawa Prefecture) in 1207.

Honen taught that people should discard all other forms of worship and concentrate solely on the chanting of Nembutsu, and this is made quite clear in his main written work, *The Selection of the Nembutsu of the Original Vow*. Honen was a spirit from the upper regions of the Bodhisattva Realm and in a past life was St. Thomas, one of Jesus' twelve disciples. The chanting of "Namu Amida Butsu" is equivalent to saying "Amen" in Christianity. Honen's guiding spirit in heaven was the spirit of St. Matthew, another of the apostles.

Matthew was himself reincarnated soon after this as Yuien, one of the followers of Shinran and famous for his work *Lamenting the Differences*. As I stated in Section 5 of Chapter Three, Honen had previously been incarnated in India as Deba, Nagarjuna's successor. I should mention, though, that Deba was not exactly the same soul as Honen; he was what is known as a brother soul.

8. The Appearance of Shinran
The next religious leader to come to the fore was Shinran (1173–1262), who is one of the greatest religious leaders of

Kamakura period (1192–1333). The sect that Honen founded is known as Jodo-shu (the Pure Land sect), and Shinran based his own philosophy on this, with his sect becoming known as the Jodo-Shinshu (the True Pure Land sect).

Shinran was the son of an aristocrat named Arinori Hino, who lived in Kyoto. At the age of nine he entered the Enryaku-ji Temple at Mt. Hiei where he studied under a high priest called Jien (1155–1225). Shinran was a brilliant student and expected by many to one day become one of the leaders of the temple. However, no matter in what esteem he was held, he felt spiritually unfulfilled and unable to attain enlightenment, so eventually, he came down from the mountain. This would have been the equivalent of an accomplished scholar who was destined to become the president of a famous university suddenly handing in his resignation, or a young top executive who was expected to take over the running of a major company suddenly leaving, and his action was the cause of much consternation among the other priests.

In 1201, at the age of twenty-eight, Shinran devoted himself to one hundred days of meditation at a temple named Rokkakudo and during this period he experienced a religious vision. He was meditating on the flame of a candle, trying to purge his mind of the impurities it had acquired while he was an elite priest on Mt. Hiei, when suddenly the flame flickered then shot up thirty centimeters (twelve inches) in height. Although he thought this a mysterious phenomenon, he did not move or break his meditation until a noble-looking man wearing the clothes of an aristocrat appeared before him. The man announced that his name was Prince Shotoku and said, "It has been my mission to watch over you for the last twenty-eight years and I have come today to inform you that you are about to reach a turning point in your life."

Shinran was amazed. Prince Shotoku had been his hero since childhood, and was the man he admired above all others. It had never occurred to him for a moment that he could have been his guiding spirit. Prince Shotoku went on to tell him that in a past life Shinran had been a disciple of Amitabha in a country in the west. Shinran took this literally, but what Prince Shotoku had really meant was that Amitabha was a way to call the power of Buddha, manifested through Jesus of Nazareth. In fact, Shinran was none other than the reincarnation of St. Paul. After informing him of the truth of his previous life, Prince Shotoku went on to say, "There is a man in this age named Honen of Yoshimizu who is preaching salvation through Amitabha. You should visit him and listen to his words; if you do, the path to enlightenment will open before you." As soon as he heard this, Shinran did as he was bidden and converted to Honen's teaching of Nembutsu.

Shinran had another spiritual experience while he was still in the Rokkakudo. Although he was an accomplished Buddhist scholar, well-versed in countless Buddhist scriptures, he had great difficulty in fighting the sin of lust. This was one of the reasons why he had felt obliged to give up his future on Mt. Hiei, but, even now, in the solitude of the Rokkakudo, he felt the pressure of carnal desire. One night, however, he saw a vision of the beautiful Kuse Kannon (Goddess of Mercy and Salvation) in his dreams. She said:

The reason why you are having so much difficulty in controlling your lust stems from the karma you formed in your previous life. You lived a life of celibacy and considered it a sin to marry. As a result, your sexual frustration became so intense that it led to epilepsy. You will soon commit the sin of having relations with a woman, but you must not be too harsh in your repentance.

I, Kuse Kannon, will allow you to embrace me. Saturate yourself in my love and use the joy that this brings you as the impetus to drive you in your mission to save the people of the world. Use your immense love to grant forgiveness to those who tremble at the thought of their sins. As Shotoku Taishi said, you are a Bodhisattva incarnate and when Kannon and Bodhisattva make love in the flesh, it produces the power to save the world.

Shinran was a fallen priest, suffering for his weakness in the face of earthly passions. He studied Nembutsu under Honen and deepened his enlightenment while following the religious ethic, similar to that of St. Paul, focusing on his feelings of guilt as a priest with the sin of lust, and salvation from this. He realized that no matter how proud a man may become of his self-endeavor, he will not win salvation; the only way to redemption is through casting one's small self at the feet of Amitabha Buddha and becoming immersed in His great love.

Shinran's absolute belief in an outside power could be explained as an interpretation of Shakyamuni's philosophy of selflessness. In fact, when considered through the medium of the concept of selflessness, Shinran's philosophy of strength from an outside power and Dogen's philosophy on the power of the self appear remarkably similar. Here lies the true meaning of Shinran's theory that evil people are the ones that Amitabha Buddha really wishes to save, which is quoted in a book by one of Shinran's followers, Yuien, entitled *Lamenting the Differences*. Shinran's work in spreading the Jodo-Shinshu (the True Pure Land sect) was inherited by Rennyo (1415–1499) who had been Andrew in a previous life, another of Jesus Christ's twelve apostles, and also from the Bodhisattva Realm.

9. Zen Buddhism—Eisai and Dogen

In contrast to the belief in an outside power of the Nembutsu sects, Zen Buddhism believed in the other extreme, the power of the self, to attain enlightenment. The Nembutsu philosophy could be described as being the "Easy Way of Practice" as one only has to chant in order to receive salvation, whereas the self-power philosophy states that actual discipline and diligence are vital if one is to achieve enlightenment, a truth that has not changed at all since the time of Shakyamuni. In the way that it demands total refinement of the self, Zen Buddhism can be described as the "Hard Way of Practice." The first advocate of the "Hard Way of Practice" was Eisai (1141–1215). He was the founder of Zen Buddhism in Japan (the Rinzai or Lin-chi sect), and he opened Ken'nin-ji Temple in Kyoto and Jufuku-ji Temple in Kamakura.

The son of a Shinto priest in Bitchu province (Okayama Prefecture), Eisai entered Enryaku-ji Temple on Mt. Hiei at the age of nineteen to study Tendai and esoteric Buddhism. Later, in 1168 and again in 1187, he visited Sung China where he studied Zen Buddhism. Upon his return in 1191, after his second sojourn, he devoted himself to advocating this new teaching, but like all the other religious innovators of this period he was forbidden from this by the conservative priests of Enryaku-ji Temple. He replied to this by publishing a work entitled *The Propagation of Zen for the Protection of the Nation* (1198).

Eisai was undoubtedly the father of Zen Buddhism in Japan, and, considering the vast influence on Japanese history and culture, it is no exaggeration to say that he was a great entrepreneur as well as a spiritual teacher. However, the Rinzai branch of Zen is what is known as Koan Zen and its real meaning was soon lost. The true purpose of Zen koans is to protect oneself from the seductions of the devil while meditating, permitting one to concentrate more deeply on exploration within. It has nothing to do with meaningless questions and answers. This original meaning has been lost and only the outer form remains today; it is really regrettable. Eisai is a high spirit who is presently living in the Brahma Realm and he too is very sad to see that only the form, not the substance, of Koan Zen remains today.

Among the followers of Eisai's disciples was a priest named Dogen (1200–1253) who was later to become the founder of the Soto (Ts'ao-t'ung in Chinese) sect of Zen Buddhism in Japan. He left his family at the age of thirteen and went to study Buddhism at Enryaku-ji Temple on Mt. Hiei. At twenty-four he visited Sung China with his teacher Myozen, who had studied under Eisai, and was taught Soto Zen by a priest named Ju-ching. Upon returning to Japan he wrote *A Universal Promotion of Zen Principles* (1227), in which he encouraged the practice of Zen, and later he produced *Discourse on the Practice of the Way* (1231) in which he made his philosophical stand clear. After this, he proceeded to write *Treasure of the True Dharma Eye*, the first systematic philosophical book to be produced in Japan.

A contemporary of Shinran, Dogen was scathing in his criticism of the Jodo sects that believed in salvation through an outside power. He likened the chanting of Nembutsu to "the sound of the frogs in the rice fields in spring." He could not stand the idea of the Latter day of Buddhist Law:

The idea of three different periods in which how precisely the Buddhist Laws are transmitted—the

True Dharma period, the Semblance Dharma period and the Decadent Dharma period—simply divided on a purely temporal basis is nothing but a method of transferring responsibility to an external agency. The true essence of the Law lies in the mind of those who practice it and is not something that can be influenced by time or circumstance.

Even in the True Dharma period when Shakyamuni was alive in this world, there were undoubtedly people whose minds were closed to enlightenment and who could not be saved. Even now in what people call the Decadent Dharma period, there exist people who are devoted to disciplining themselves in their thought and action and who can possibly attain enlightenment. To proclaim that this is the period of the degeneration of the Law and provoke the fear of hell in the minds of people with the sole purpose of converting people is to mistake the means for the end.

As long as a person is sound in body and capable of distinguishing between right and wrong, they are capable of attaining enlightenment through spiritual discipline. Whatever happens, we must not stray from the fundamental principle of Buddhist training. And what is this fundamental principle? It is that enlightenment is not something that lies at the end of a long discipline; rather, enlightenment exists within the discipline. In fact, discipline is itself enlightenment. It is not good enough to simply sit back and wish for rebirth in paradise. No matter how unskillful you may be, you must be determined to practice discipline and walk the true path of Buddhism.

What I have reported here is Dogen's philosophy. While it is true that he was a poet, philosopher and seeker of the Law at its highest level, he failed to realize that there are two sides to human discipline—although humans must strive to raise themselves to the highest level and seek perfection, they must also live for the love of others. People cannot be saved through the chanting of Nembutsu alone, but, at the same time, it must be remembered that a deep human love lies in the background of all the Nembutsu sects. Dogen is presently living in the middle area of the Bodhisattva Realm where he is disciplining himself in love. One cannot enter the highest part of the Bodhisattva Realm without manifesting love.

Apart from these two masters of Zen, there was also Muso Soseki (1275–1351) who was in fact the brother soul of T'ien-t'ai Chih-i. He worked hard for the furtherance of Buddhism and, like T'ien-t'ai Chih-i, was a skilled politician as well as a priest. His followers are said to number over thirteen thousand.

10. Nichiren Roars Out

I have talked at length about several great priests of thirteenth century, but no discussion of the religion of this period could be complete without mention of Nichiren (1222–1282). Born in Kominato in the province of Awa (Chiba Prefecture), he went to study Buddhism at the nearby Kiyosumi-dera temple at the age of twelve. He was given the name Rencho when he was ordained at sixteen and devoted himself to studying Jodo (Pure Land) Buddhism. Later he traveled to Kamakura and Enryaku-ji Temple on Mt. Hiei where he studied the Tendai Eshin tradition. During this period he had the opportunity to read numerous Buddhist texts and was particularly influenced by the work of T'ien-t'ai Chih-i and Saicho.

Nichiren returned to Kiyosumi-dera Temple in 1252 and the following year he discovered what he felt to be the true essence of Buddhism contained within the Lotus Sutra. He founded a new sect based on this knowledge, but his total devotion to the Lotus Sutra and antagonistic attitude toward all other sects won him the antipathy of the Nembutsu priests in the temple as well as that of the Tojo family who ruled the area at the time. As a result, he was driven out of the temple. Fleeing to Kamakura, which was the de facto capital of the country at this time, his hostility toward all other sects grew and was summed up in his four aphorisms: "Nembutsu leads to the hell of incessant suffering," "Zen is the teaching of the devil," "Shingon will ruin the country," and "Ritsu are all traitors." At the same time, he preached that the Lotus Sutra was the only true Law, the Right Law, and that a devotion to its teachings would guarantee salvation for the individual and peace for the country.

Between 1257 and 1260 there were numerous earthquakes in eastern Japan, coupled with severe famines, which Nichiren put down to the dominance of evil faiths. He prophesied that unless people cast these heresies aside, the country would be wracked by conflict within the country and invasion from outside. In 1260, he completed his *On Securing the Peace of the Land through the Propagation of True Buddhism*, which he presented to Tokiyori Hojo, the de facto ruler of the country. This resulted in Nichiren's exile to Izu in 1261. Even after he was allowed to return, he continued to suffer from oppression and persecution by the Tojo family, eventually being banished to the Isle of Sado. However, after this, Japan was attacked twice by a Mongol invasion force, just as Nichiren had foretold (although both attempts were repelled, contrary to his prophesy), and the government, frightened by this apparent display of supernatural power, decided to let him leave his place of exile. While Nichiren had been living in Sado, he wrote *Opening of the Eyes* and *The True Object of Worship*, in which he taught that the chanting of the words "Namu Myoho Renge Kyo" (taking refuge in the Lotus Sutra) would guarantee salvation.

I would now like to evaluate Nichiren's teachings from the perspective of the Truth over a seven-hundred-year history. First, looking at its fanatic, exclusionist, self-righteous and closed character, his sect could well be described as a forerunner of the apocalyptic cults of today. Secondly, there was his exclusive emphasis on the Lotus Sutra. He claimed that only the Lotus Sutra transmitted the Truth and that all other sutras or scriptures were false, but he was mistaken; there are thousands of gateways to the Truth, often referred to as "eighty-four thousand gateways." As is the case in the Bible, each of the sutras were written at a later period by disciples, so it is only to be expected that some of them fail to transmit Shakyamuni Buddha's teachings precisely. It is widely accepted among academic circles that the Lotus Sutra was not written until four to five hundred years after the death of Shakyamuni and as such it only reflects a single facet of his teaching. All of the sutras are a record of the conversations between Shakyamuni and his disciples; therefore, they are influenced by the time, place and people involved, making it impossible for any one of them to be considered true to the exclusion of all others.

Next we come to his attacks on the other sects, and these can be said to have both their good and bad points. On the plus side one can say that they created the impetus for the feverish activities for which the Nichiren sect is renowned. People who would preach the Truth must be seen to overflow with energy, or their message will not spread. The more convinced they become that they have found the ultimate Truth, the more other faiths appear to be false. This is not restricted to the Nichiren sect and is equally true of Christianity. There is only one teaching, only one truth, but when it is explained in numerous ways by numerous people, the spiritually immature become easily confused and think that each differs from the others. What it boils down to is that the disciples, unlike the founder, are only capable of comprehending the parts.

Therefore, to put it simply, Kukai's esoteric Shingon sect, Shinran's True Pure-Land sect, Dogen's Zen and Nichiren's Lotus Sutra all represent different gateways to the Truth, all of which had been incorporated in Shakyamuni's teachings. By reading *The Laws of the Sun* and my other writings, it will then become obvious that Nichiren's method of exclusively chanting "Namu Myoho Renge Kyo" runs contrary to Buddha's true intention. Nichiren's attack on the other sects can be understood as stemming from his eagerness to spread the Truth, but in branding them all false he was very much mistaken. Shinran and Dogen were both high spirits, just as Nichiren himself was.

In order to gain a full understanding of Nichiren's ideology and behavior, it is necessary for us to look also at the fruit that his sect has produced. First there is Soka Gakkai, which poses as the lay organization of the Nichiren Shoshu (although it has already been excommunicated by the priests of the Head Temple) and is in fact a false and heretical religious movement. This organization was founded on mistaken principles. The second president, Josei Toda, who in influence exceeds the founder, was in serious financial trouble and decided to become a false evangelist to collect money, taking advantage of the creed of Nichiren sect that all people have to do to be saved is chanting "Namu Myoho Renge Kyo." When he discovered that he was making even more money than he could ever have imagined, he gave up his business as a loan shark to become a full-time man of religion. The presidency passed from Toda to the present leader, Daisaku Ikeda, who strengthened the order's money-making potential, adding the slogan of "World Peace" to his creed while exploiting the Taisekiji Honzan Temple as a religious figurehead and forming the political party, called Komeito, to represent him in government. This story can be compared to that of, for example, a taxi company president who constructs a statue of Kannon (Goddess of Mercy) and creates a religious body as a method of avoiding paying taxes.

Nichiren completely abandoned the quest of personal perfection and concentrated only on the salvation of the masses, although both are essential aspects of Buddhism. Soka Gakkai took this as justification for altering the character of his teachings from mercy to depravity. That is why their believers do not hesitate to use such tactics as wire tapping, following or threatening those who criticize the cult's activities, setting dogs on them, or sending them the dead bodies of snakes or birds or slabs of bloody meat— actions that are the antithesis of everything that Buddhism stands for. However, they believe that all they have to do is chant "Namu Myoho Renge Kyo" and they will be redeemed. Conscience and the Buddhist precepts mean nothing whatsoever to them. It is said that Japanese Buddhism has failed to produce any outstanding priest since Nichiren, but the truth is that there has been a never-ending succession of people who preached that salvation can be won through the chanting of a particular phrase or word. The enlightenment and wisdom that lay at the basis of Shakyamuni's preaching have been forgotten, replaced by a philosophy of divine favor and brain-washed fanaticism that continues to grow.

When Nichiren's philosophy is utilized to create a simple political philosophy, there is very little to differentiate it from Marxism. Marxism claimed that the end justified the means, which led inevitably to state terror and purges. In the same way, if the corrupted Tendai Hongaku philosophy, which preaches that chanting will atone for any sin, were to transmogrified into political power, it would create an insane totalitarianism.

We must not allow the creation of a future society run by the members of Soka Gakkai in which bugging, surveillance, betrayal, and unjust imprisonment become the norm. At all costs, we must avoid Japan becoming like the Soviet Union, where people were afraid to speak without first checking under the table for a listening apparatus. We must hold firm to the position of enlightenment and wisdom.

Chapter Five
When Love Surges Forward

1. Beginning with Love

In Chapters Two, Three, and Four, I have expounded on the history of the high spirits who appeared in the West, the East and Japan respectively. My aim in this book is to try and present an overall history of the deeds of the high spirits, a unique effort that has never been attempted in the past and may never be achieved again in the future.

I could quite easily write the history of humankind covering the last ten, thousand, hundred thousand or even one million years. Of course, this is not the kind of knowledge that is likely to reside within the brain cells of this man whom you know as Ryuho Okawa, so how is it that I am capable of achieving such a task? It is because this knowledge exists in the eighty percent of my soul that still resides in the ninth dimension.

All this aside, even if I were to write the entire history of the human race, it would not have much significance for the average person. As you know, what is generally thought of as history are the events of the last few thousand years, the deeds of the high spirits who have come down to do Buddha's will, and these are what must be remembered in order that they be passed on down to future generations. For this reason, I will not even attempt to trace the entire course of history in this chapter; rather, I will concentrate on the deeds of those prophets who I think are worthy of particular attention. These are people who have been entrusted with the mission to carry out the thought and teachings of Buddha in some concrete way. They are Zeus and Apollo from Greece; Moses, Elijah and Jesus Christ from among the Jews; Mohammed from the Middle East and, more recently, Kanzo Uchimura, Masaharu Taniguchi and Shinji Takahashi from modern Japan. Of course I have not been able to include everybody; there have been many other great prophets throughout history whose deeds make it very difficult not to include them in this list, but I will just focus on the most important.

The end of the twentieth century was a turning point for humanity and the nine people I have listed here are those whose teachings need to be passed on to future generations. For this reason, it does not matter that they have been superficially divided into Christians, Muslims, Jews and Shintoists; the important thing is that they were trying to convey the will of Buddha to the people of their time.

The history of humankind is not a product of chance; at the core of each period we can find prophets who are acting as the messengers from higher reaches of the heavenly realm. It is irrelevant whether or not their true value was apparent to others at the time; what is important is that they never cease to influence others for hundreds or thousands of years. To put it another way, the history of humankind's civilizations and cultures is based on the works of a handful of prophets. It is a fact that Buddha sends down a prophet to Earth every hundred or thousand years and it should be realized that this is a token of Buddha's great love toward us.

That a prophet appears in a particular age is the ultimate proof of Buddha's love. The different ages are begun by the prophets and it is their work that creates them. As the prophets are symbols of Buddha's great love, it can be said that the history of the human race began with love, and in the surging wave of Buddha's love that is presently rushing toward us, we can feel the beginning of a new age.

2. Zeus

The first prophet I would like to discuss is Zeus, the principle god of the Greek pantheon. He was born approximately three thousand six hundred years ago, that is to say in the seventeenth century B.C., on the Aegean island of Crete. Approximately eight hundred years before Zeus' time, Hermes, who was a part of the Buddha consciousness, lived and preached in Greece. Hermes preached a Truth that was rich in artistic values, but his teachings had fallen into decay and were no longer heeded by the people. Greece is blessed with beautiful scenery, clear blue skies and the mysterious marine blue waters of the Mediterranean, and this is reflected in the people, who are generally cheerful and open-minded. But at around the time that Zeus was born, the countries that made up the area were becoming unsettled and rumor of war was in the air.

Zeus was born into one of the royal houses and at the age of twenty-two, married Hera. There was nothing about him to set him apart from other princes of that time, although he had shown a strong interest in music from an early age. However, from about the time he married Hera, a change started to come over him. Hera had well-developed psychic powers and was particularly talented at precognition. This proved very useful for Zeus as he was able to approach the battles in which he was involved with a knowledge of events that allowed him to turn them in his favor.

He became fascinated with his wife's gift and took to participating in her séances until, at the age of twenty-seven, he too was visited with a spiritual awakening. At this time, his guiding spirit was Hermes, who was later to return to Earth as Shakyamuni. Once he had acquired supernatural powers of his own, Zeus built a special spirit chamber in the temple. Its columns and floor were of marble and in the center was a fountain with a marble statue of Hermes with sapphire eyes. When Zeus knelt and prayed in the chamber, the eyes of the statue started to shine and the spirit of Hermes would appear in front of Zeus, in all its shining glory. Hermes wore a golden crown and in his right hand he held a flute that shone with rainbow-colored light. His whole body was covered in pure, thin, white silk and at his waist was a brown, diamond-studded belt with a buckle engraved in the shape of a lion and a deer. The lion represented courage while the deer stood for art.

Sometimes Hermes would offer Zeus political advice, but most of their time together was spent discussing the mysteries of heaven. When Hermes did not have anything in particular to talk about, he would simply play his flute for about ten minutes until he disappeared once more. When they were talking, he would teach Zeus about spiritual emancipation, explaining how people everywhere were bound with chains of their own making, believing that the physical body was everything as they lived their lives with an extremely limited self-perception. Hermes wanted to free these people from their narrow world vision, to awaken them to the Truth and teach them to live with a bright and cheerful philosophy. These were his main aims.

Zeus had two brothers named Poseidon and Hades. Zeus was in control of the army while command of his navies fell to Poseidon. These navies boasted several thousand ships and almost two hundred thousand sailors, making them invincible at sea. Poseidon was a realist and became very impatient with his elder brother who advanced or withdrew his armies in accordance with Hera's psychic knowledge. In his opinion the army should crush its enemies when it had the opportunity and, to his eyes, the gentle Zeus looked indecisive and weak. Feeling that Hera stood between his brother and full command of the armed forces, Poseidon attempted to assassinate her, but failed.

This act, however, led to a rift between the army and navy and after a fierce battle, Zeus was triumphant and Poseidon ruined.

Hades also possessed psychic power but was jealous of the way that the people all looked up to Zeus and Hera; he determined therefore to find a way to prove that he was the greatest psychic in the whole country. Eventually, the devil found its way into Hades' mind. He gathered around him many psychics who were possessed by evil spirits, in a way that is very reminiscent of several of the new religions that have sprung up around the world in recent years. He claimed to be able to communicate with God and pass on His messages, when in fact the words came from the devil. Hades went as far as becoming a genuine threat to Zeus' mission to spread the Truth, so eventually Zeus had no alternative but to make battle with Hades' army and cast him down.

Needless to say, all this fighting with his own brothers took its toll on Zeus and his guardian spirit, Asert, who was later to be incarnated as Amoghavajra, had to step in and help calm the agonies of his conscience. Zeus is a being from the Cosmic Realm of the ninth dimension, and is presently acting as the god of literature, music and art.

3. The Shining One, Apollo

Apollo was the son of Zeus. He inherited his mother's good looks (in Greek mythology, his mother is said to be Leto) and was a radiant youth much loved both in the palace and throughout the kingdom for his angelic demeanor. Athena was Apollo's sister and three years his elder. (In Greek mythology she was said to be the daughter of Zeus and Metis, the goddess of discretion. She was later reincarnated as the Austrian Empress Maria Theresa, (1717–1780). Athena was very much a tomboy in her youth and from the age of sixteen she took to wearing armor and leading her father's troops in battle. She was twenty-three and Apollo twenty when their father died at the age of forty-seven. A stray arrow had struck Zeus in the left side during a battle and the wound became infected, leading to his death three months later.

Upon the death of Zeus, the family retainers became very worried. For all that Athena was a valiant leader in battle, she was still only a girl of twenty-three and her brother Apollo showed no inclination to interest himself with affairs of state or war. He was a very refined young man and spent all his time exploring his inner world. Eventually, Athena settled the matter herself, declaring that she would take command of the armies. All the retainers then pledged their fealty to her. Apollo took this opportunity to leave the palace, climbing Mt. Olympus where the gods were said to gather. He took up the life of a seeker of Truth, living in a cave and devoting himself to spiritual discipline.

He spent his days in meditation and introspection. He reflected upon his childhood when he was much loved by his parents; he remembered how he would quarrel with his sister and watch the statesmen, some pure and loyal, others scheming for their own gain. He had never been able to play like a normal child and remembered having been very taken by the mystic phenomena he had witnessed in the presence of his parents. In this way, he recalled the memories of the past, and examined each occurrence from an unbiased viewpoint, as if from someone else's. Eventually, on a beautiful starlit night approximately one month after he started his meditation, his late father appeared before him and spoke:

Apollo, I have left this world now and live in a land of gold where all the people are pure in heart and live together in harmony. When I was alive, I used to believe that humans consisted of a body and a soul and that it was important to maintain the harmony between the two. However, now I have returned to heaven, I realize that I was wrong; there are not two parts to a person, only the soul.

The body is no more than a shadow of the soul and, looked at from the standpoint of eternal life, the period we spend on Earth passes in a blink of an eye. The body is simply a vehicle for the soul for this briefest of moments and the people who devote themselves to physical desire or to extending their time on Earth are to be pitied. Wars are such futile things; the winner is fighting for his life but it is a fight that can know no real victory. The victors will die eventually and, when they return to this side, they will repent having spent their whole lives in strife.

Our family will be destroyed within the next few decades, the palace will be thrown down and Athena will be defeated in battle, but you must not worry. As of today, you will become endowed with spiritual powers that will allow you to communicate with the high spirits. Find your own way, consulting with those high spirits. I want you to preach spiritual teachings to save people. You must do this for both of our sakes.

As was promised, Apollo received spiritual gifts that allowed him to communicate freely with the high spirits in heaven. He created a religious order that started from Mt. Olympus, which later expanded to Delos and Delphi. In the Real World, Apollo is one of the seven archangels and is named Michael. He was incarnated on Earth three thousand six hundred years ago in Greece and preached the message of Light. Later he was to appear in Israel in the time of King Jeroboam, son of Joash, as the prophet Amos.

4. Enter Moses

About four hundred years after the passing of Apollo there was a movement among the inhabitants of the heavenly realm to build a Kingdom of God on Earth in a concrete form. To this end, a great leader was sent down from the ninth dimension to Egypt. This was Moses. He was born the son of a Hebrew slave, but soon after his birth he was set adrift on the river Nile in a reed basket. Luckily he was discovered by the pharaoh's daughter and raised in the palace where he was engaged in both warfare and academic studies. However, when he reached the age of eighteen, he discovered that he was in fact the child of a slave.

This knowledge caused him endless suffering. At this time, vast numbers of slaves were toiling to build the city of Ramses in commemoration of the reign of Ramses II (1292–1225 B.C.). Moses realized that but for an accident of fate he would be suffering with them instead of living a life of leisure in the palace. He continued to devote himself to his studies while he waited for the day when he could lead his fellow countrymen to freedom. His planned exodus from Egypt happened during the reign of the pharaoh Merenptah (reigned 1225–1215 B.C.), and this could be described as a sort of coup d'état. He had waited seventeen years for his chance and he was now thirty-five years old.

His rebel army gradually grew, freeing slaves to swell their numbers even further until there were six hundred thousand able-bodied men among their ranks. However, Moses did not plan armed insurrection; all he wanted was to lead the Hebrew people away so that they could found their own nation. He was concerned that his huge army would turn into a mob that would ruin the kingdom and so he gathered them all together to try and escape from the country in what was to become known as the Exodus.

Moses could not forget an experience he had had at the age of twenty-seven. At the time, he was living disguised as a shepherd while he studied under his father-in-law, a priest of Midian named Jethro. One day he was looking out over the fields when suddenly a pillar of flame appeared before him. He walked up to it and heard a voice. "Moses, remove your shoes," it said, appearing to come from the heart of the flame itself. "I am who I am. I existed before all else. I am the God of Abraham, the God of Isaac, the God of Jacob-Israel. I am the Lord of all the armies, I am Yahweh. Save my people in Egypt. Listen to the sorrows of my people. Moses, free my people, deliver them out of Egypt and take them to the land flowing with milk and honey. Lead them to Canaan and build the nation of Israel. To this end have I selected you."

Guided by the voice of Yahweh, who is also sometimes described as Jehovah, Moses led his six hundred thousand men, together with women and children totaling almost two million, out of Egypt. However, just as they reached the Red Sea they saw the pharaoh's armies chasing them in hot pursuit. Moses built an altar by the sea and prayed to Yahweh.

"O my Lord, I have led the Hebrew nation out of Egypt as you commanded but, as you know, our way forward is blocked by the sea and the king's army is at our heels. I do not have the ships to carry all our people and if I fight the king's army, many of our people will be killed or wounded. Please, O Lord of the armies, save us from our enemies."

"Moses, why do you fear? There is nothing in this world that I do not control. The wind, the trees, the mountains, the rivers and the sky are all at my command. Look, where is this sea that you fear? For the sake of my people, I will sunder it apart." No sooner did Yahweh speak than an unbelievable phenomenon took place before the eyes of Moses and the Hebrews. The sea split for a length of two kilometers (one and one-quarter mile), leaving a path twelve meters (forty feet) wide across the sea floor. As if they were held back by an invisible wall, the waters reared to a height of fifteen meters (fifty feet) on either side to fall back again upon themselves. Here and there along the newly formed path, red and blue fish of various sizes could be seen flopping around helplessly on the sea floor.

"Hurry!" cried Moses, and the Hebrew people needed no further urging. They ran down the newly formed path and after they had passed, the waters of the sea came crashing back to reclaim what was theirs. Part of the pharaoh's army was drowned, and the others, seeing what had happened, fled the scene in fear.

On the top of Mt. Sinai, another miracle happened. Yahweh appeared before Moses again and revealed to him the Ten Commandments:

1. You shall have no other gods before me.
2. You shall not make any graven image.
3. You shall not take the name of the Lord your God in vain.

4. You shall remember the Sabbath day and keep it holy.
5. You shall honor your father and mother.
6. You shall not kill.
7. You shall not commit adultery.
8. You shall not steal.
9. You shall not bear false witness against your neighbor.
10. You shall not covet your neighbor's house.

The first four commandments are religious, the fifth is moral and the sixth to tenth are ethical and legal precepts. The Ten Commandments had great influence over the years that followed in that they founded the idea of a personal God and monotheism, and that they aimed to control social order through divine law.

Yahweh was a spirit from the ninth dimension named Enlil. However, the confusion between Elohim (the god of El), who was worshiped widely in the Middle East, and Moses' guiding spirit, Yahweh, began at this time and was to lead to a history of persecution, the isolation of Israel, and fierce wars for the following three thousand years. It is unfortunate that Moses was unable to differentiate between the supreme God, El, and the numerous spirits that surrounded Him. This would prove the source of a terrible tragedy in the centuries to come.

5. Elijah, the Fighter

Moses was followed by Elijah, who came to establish the faith in Yahweh. He was a man with an indomitable personality and his fighting spirit reminds us of the thirteenth-century Japanese priest, Nichiren, whom I spoke about in the previous chapter. Elijah appeared more than two thousand eight hundred years ago, during the time when King Ahab (reigned 874–852 B.C.) ruled over the northern kingdom of Israel. Ahab was the son of King Omri (reigned 886–874 B.C.) and was said to be the most active leader of the Omri dynasty. Ahab was particularly skilled in war and diplomacy; he formed an alliance with the Phoenician city of Tyre, marrying Jezebel, the daughter of Ethbaal, King of Tyre.

In those days, Phoenicia was located along the Mediterranean coast of Palestine. Its people were noted for their navigational skills that resulted in their growing rich from the sea trade. Having befriended the city of Tyre, Ahab's kingdom also flourished, its economy growing rapidly and in many ways resembling that of contemporary Japan.

However, financial wealth led to a rise in materialism and the worship of Baal, the god of wealth, became very popular. Baalism was a form of idolatry and the people all kept small statues of Baal in their homes, while Ahab afforded the Baalist priests a rank equivalent to that of present-day civil servants. The merchant class, which had grown spectacularly with the nation's new-found status as a trade center, tended to favor Baalism while the farmers, who preserved the old ways of life, remained loyal to the God Yahweh. It was against this background that Elijah appeared in the role of religious reformer. At the age of twenty-one he received a revelation from Yahweh and learning of his mission began to gather a band of believers around him.

When he was twenty-five, Elijah rose up in action. He stated that Baal was a false god and belief in this cult was destroying the traditional monotheism of Yahweh. He approached Ahab and asked to be allowed to challenge the Baalist priests, who were under the protection of Jezebel, to decide once and for all which god was true. Ahab gave his approval and gathered together four hundred and fifty Baalist prophets, telling them that it should be determined, in a public place, which was the true god, Elijah's Yahweh or their Baal.

It was decided that Elijah and the four hundred and fifty Baalist priests should meet on the top of Mt. Carmel. Two piles of wood were stacked up and on each was placed a bull for sacrifice. Neither side was to light the fire themselves, but to pray to their respective god to act for them. Elijah turned to his adversaries and said, "Call upon your god. I shall call mine, Yahweh. The one who answers with fire shall be accepted as the true God."

The four hundred and fifty priests called out to their god from morning until noon, but no fire appeared in answer to their pleas. Eventually, they took to dancing around their altar, and cutting each other with swords to add blood to their prayers, but Baal did not heed them.

Finally, Elijah went up to his own altar and said, "Hear me, O Lord, show the people that you are the one and only true God. Let them turn their hearts away from their evil faith." No sooner had he spoken than a single bolt of lightening streaked down from the south-west and struck Elijah's sacrifice, setting it alight instantly. The prophets of Baal looked on in dismay as the fire consumed the wood, the bull, the stone and dust of the altar, and even the water in a ditch surrounding the site. The people who had witnessed all this believed once more in Yahweh and, acting on Elijah's command, they rounded up the false prophets and executed them on the banks of the Kishon.

This is not fiction; it is a historical fact. Yahweh caused this phenomenon to happen in order that the people could realize the mistake of worshipping Baal, also known as Beelzebub, and return to Israel's own religion. This episode shows us that heaven is prepared to take extreme measures in order to keep the flame of Truth burning. Elijah left this world at the age of twenty-eight and is now living in the Tathagata Realm of the eighth dimension where he is in charge of planning for the entire Earth.

6. Jesus Christ, the Savior

Numerous prophets were incarnated on Earth to continue the movement to create a kingdom of God in Israel. Considering the numbers of high spirits who were incarnated there, it is hardly surprising that the people of the Jewish race consider that they had been selected by God, that they were His chosen people.

Elijah was followed by numerous Guiding Spirits of Light including Amos, Isaiah, Jeremiah, Elisha, Ezekiel and

Daniel. The teachings they left were then compiled in the Old Testament of the Bible. From about 100 B.C. the belief that the Messiah would be born among the people became widespread and found many followers. According to the prophesies, the Messiah would come down to Earth and create the Kingdom of God, but would be hung on the cross, killed, and then be resurrected.

In those days, there were numerous separate sects among God's followers: the Pharisees, who preached strict adherence to the Ten Commandments; the Sadducees, who represented the conservative majority; and the Essenes, who looked for the coming of the Messiah. Two members of this last sect were Joseph, age thirty-six, and Mary, seventeen, who gave birth to a boy named Immanuel, who was later to become known as Jesus Christ.

In the same way that Shakyamuni Buddha was said to have sprung from the armpit of Queen Maya, there is a widespread belief that Jesus was born of a virgin. The story was, in fact, put about by followers of Jesus' disciples who wished to give him godly status as the Messiah, but the truth is that he was born in the normal way through wedlock. However, it is a historical fact that three astrologers of the East consulted the stars and prophesied that the Messiah would be born in Nazareth.

By the time he was seven, Jesus had already been visited by an angel and given the gifts of spiritual speech, spiritual sight (clairvoyance) and spiritual hearing (clairaudience). An angel had entered his body resulting in his being able to hold eloquent discussions on the Old Testament while still only a young child. This amazed the members of his church and by the time he was ten years old the air was full of rumors that he was a child prodigy. The leaders of the Essenes realized that he must be the Messiah who had been prophesied in the Old Testament. They decided that they had to protect him from the other sects and to bring him up most carefully.

Although the stories of Jesus' childhood appear to have been carefully excised from the original Bible, he was raised as a member of the religious elite. According to what I have been able to learn in the spirit world, at the age of thirteen he was taken by a young Essene priest to Egypt for one year to study various religions. When he was sixteen, several priests, including some of the church elders, took him on a trip to west India where he learned to meditate through the traditional yoga techniques and was able to study various Buddhist scriptures.

What he gained from his sojourn in India was the ability to create physical miracles through willpower and mastery of the mysterious power that can be attained through prayer. In India, he studied under a mystic named Manitula, who taught him the secret of how to materialize fish and loaves of bread from thin air. This is a skill known as a "materialization phenomenon." With regard to philosophy, he was fascinated by the altruistic practices and offerings of Buddhism. All in all, he studied in India for approximately eighteen months.

When Jesus reached twenty-one he traveled again, this time to Persia where he studied the dualism of good and evil as preached in Zoroastrianism. He did a great deal of research into Ahura Mazda, the supreme god of Zoroaster, but was not impressed by the fire-worship ceremonies. From about the age of twenty-five, Jesus concentrated on his studies of the Old Testament, and from the age of twenty-seven spent three years in the cave of Qumran near the Dead Sea where he practiced meditation and austerities. It was at this time that he built the framework for his future teachings. He considered that the Buddhist law of karma—"reap what you sow"—was important, and decided to emphasize the teaching of love that he felt was rather lacking in Buddhism. He felt that he would also be able to utilize the spiritual power of the yogis as a method of waking the people of the world, while from the Zoroastrians he adopted the idea of driving out evil. In this way, his philosophy gradually took shape.

When he was thirty years old, the Angel of Light, Gabriel, came to him in his cave and spoke the following: "Return to Nazareth. On the way you will meet a man named John who is baptizing people in the waters of the Jordan. He is known among the people as John the Baptist. Your meeting with him will mark the beginning of your ministry on Earth. After this, spiritually related people will find you and become your disciples. They will be twelve in number and will become the principle followers of your teachings."

Jesus' teachings in the years that followed are approximately recorded in the Bible. In particular, the teaching of love by one of El Cantare's brother souls, Hermes, had a strong impact on Jesus' spiritual awakening. It was this that gave Jesus' message its universality and held the key to his teachings becoming a world religion.

Jesus taught for only about three years, which was a very short time, but the knowledge he had acquired in the twenty-three years since his spiritual awakening was such that everybody was amazed at its profundity. He died at the age of thirty-three on the cross at Golgotha, but the man who died there was to continue to shape world history for the next two thousand years.

Jesus' main difficulty lay in the fact that he had to try and alter the old belief in Yahweh, which had degenerated into an egotistic tribal religion, and move the people on to a new belief in the universal God (El Cantare)—a break with tradition that was to earn him the enmity of the conservatives in the Church. On the other hand, the extreme suffering experienced by his followers in the Roman Empire in the years following, starting with the martyrdom of Peter (64 A.D.) and Paul (67 A.D.), was due to the clash between the multiple deities of the Greco-Roman tradition and the monotheism of Christianity. However, if the people had realized the relationship between the Ultimate God, El Cantare, and the multiple gods, this kind of tragedy could have been avoided. Jesus Christ is presently one of the

highest spirits in the ninth dimension who share the ultimate responsibilities for the Earth.

7. Mohammed

Mohammed (Muhammad) was born in 570 A.D. in Mecca,
an important trading city in western Arabia. Almost five
hundred and forty years had passed since the death of Jesus
Christ. In those days, Mecca was controlled by the Quraish
tribe and Mohammed was born into a minor branch of it,
the Hashim clan. Mohammed's father died before he was
born and his mother, Aminah, died when he was only six
years old, leaving him an orphan. He went to live with his
grandfather Abdul Muttalib, and after he died he was taken
in by his father's younger brother, Abu Talib. This all
resulted in his childhood being very hard.

At the age of twenty-five, Mohammed married a beautiful, rich widow of forty, named Khadijah, who owned a
trade caravan, and they were blessed with three sons and
four daughters. Mohammed spent the next fifteen years
living the life of a rich merchant, but fate had another plan
in store for him.

It was his practice to spend a certain part of the year
meditating and praying in a cave in the mountains approximately five kilometers (three miles) north-east of Mecca.

One night in 610 (it is called the "Lailat-al-Qadr"),
when Mohammed was forty years old, he had an overpow-
ering spiritual experience in a cave on Mt. Hira during the
month of Ramadan. A solemn voice rang out through the

cave and a luminous being grasped him by the throat, telling him to remember the words of God that would be revealed to him and later make a record of them. Mohammed was terrified; he thought himself possessed by one of the evil djinns of the desert and tried to avoid his fate. However, encouraged by his wife Khadijah, he gradually came to accept his mission, and from about 613 he began to preach to the people. Khadijah was very supportive of his message and became his first convert.

Later, after talking to Khadijah's cousin, Waraqa, who was a Christian, as well as to several Jews, Mohammed came to believe that the being who had spoken to him was named Jibril, the archangel Gabriel of Christian lore. The name of the one and only god in Islam, Allah, is not a proper noun as such; it is a general term meaning "god of creation" who had been worshipped on the Arabian peninsula for a long time. This can be seen in the fact that Mohammed's father's name was Abd Allah (servant of God), or Abdullah in a simplified form. If we were to find the name of the Middle-Eastern god of creation, it would be Elohim, in other words, El Cantare. In this respect, Mohammed shared the same mission as the Jewish or Christian prophets and this illustrates the magnanimity of El Cantare toward humankind.

Mohammed received numerous revelations, which he passed on to the rest of humankind, and these were written down during the reign of the third caliph, Uthman, to produce the one hundred and fourteen chapters of the Koran

(Qur'an). His teachings can be summed up under six themes: Allah the one and only god, angels, scriptures, prophets, the life after death, and predestination.

Mohammed had been strongly influenced by the Jews and Christians he met during his travels as a merchant in Syria and this resulted in him denying the idolatry of the Meccans who worshipped the sun, stars and rocks. His new religion spread like wildfire, finding eager supporters among the poor and the slaves. However, they were persecuted by the Quraish tribe who ruled Mecca both politically and religiously. Eventually, Mohammed was banished from Mecca in 622, after which he went to live in Medina (which was then called Yathrib). This move is known among Muslims as the Hijrah (meaning emigration) and marks the first year of the Muslim calendar. After this, Mohammed organized his religious order and in 630 he led his forces back and conquered Mecca with the intention of unifying the Arab peoples.

Mohammed was a spirit from the Tathagata Realm of the eighth dimension. The messages he received in the cave originated from the same group of high spirits who had guided Jesus and the Old Testament prophets. However, they differed in detail due to the fact that Mohammed was preaching in an area that was based on a merchant economy and that he was able to command a powerful military force. This illustrates the powerful influence that period and location can have on the same basic message. Also, the teachings listed in the Koran focused on worship, fasting and precepts that resulted in Islam gradually becoming a formalized religion and caused it to lose its original message. As he did not have the chance of undergoing extensive religious training as Jesus did, Mohammed was unable to receive the type of revelations that could be developed into spiritual teachings. On top of this, his political and military power led him to stress the importance of the Jihad, the holy war, which eventually resulted in a legacy of strife among Muslims that exists to this day. Even in the present day the Middle-East remains covered by a thick fog of negative thought energy.

Finally, the fact that Muslims came to regard Allah, who had been the most revered among many gods, as the one and only god, neglecting all others, remains one of the strongest characteristics of Islam. I am sure the reader will have realized that this is not quite right, considering the multi-dimensional structure of the Real World. This is what led to the war with the Quraish people, who also worshipped Allah as their highest deity, because it meant the denial of all their other gods who had also been worshipped at the Kaaba. However, regardless of whether or not he was correct in what he preached, Mohammed's creed of a single god, casting aside all previous beliefs, is meaningful in that it represented a major innovation in religion.

After the death of Khadijah, Mohammed took more than ten new wives, including his favorite, Aisha. In addition to this historical fact, the Muslim practice of taking multiple wives caused some Christians to consider Islam an evil religion. However, it should be realized that all the religious wars in which Islam became embroiled created a large number of orphans and widows, that polygamy thus formed a type of basic social security, and that rules were laid down to govern the husband's duty to treat each wife equally.

8. The Faith of Kanzo Uchimura

We will now move to Japan and look at the life of a prophet who appeared in recent history, Kanzo Uchimura (1861–1930). He was a leading figure in the Christian church from the end of the nineteenth century and it would be no exaggeration to say that it was due to his effort that the faith took root in Japan. He was born at the end of the feudal period into a low-class samurai family in the Takasaki domain (present day Gunma Prefecture). In 1877 he entered the Sapporo Agricultural College in Hokkaido and, being deeply influenced by the teachings of Dr. William Clark, decided to be baptized. Inazo Nitobe also attended this college at the same time.

In 1884, Uchimura entered Amherst University in the United States, and after returning to Japan he taught history at the First Higher Middle School. However, he refused to bow down to the Imperial Rescript on Education and was dismissed from his position for disrespect. After that, he wandered around the country, from Kyoto and Osaka to Kumamoto, in much the same position as Dante had been after he had been banished from Florence. In 1897 he became the English language editor-in-chief of the *Yorozu*

Choho newspaper, but was forced to leave due to his antiwar stance. After publishing the *Tokyo Independent Magazine*, Uchimura worked from his home in Kashiwagi and continued to produce the *Biblical Studies* magazine. In his later years, he founded "The Second Advent of Christ Movement," holding lectures throughout the country. His most famous works are *Consolations of a Christian, Seeking Peace of Mind*, and *How I Became a Christian*.

It is great to have a man with such a great spiritual strength appearing in modern Japan. Obviously his spirit belonged to the Christian spirit group and his aim during his life on Earth was the spread of Christianity within Japan, but his legacy is something much greater than that.

First, there is his concept of Non-church Christianity. In Europe, Martin Luther said, "Man is justified by his faith alone," rebelling against the established Catholic Church and founding Protestantism around an exclusive faith in the Bible. However, Uchimura went even further, preaching that the possession of faith alone was sufficient and stressing the direct connection between conscience and God.

Second, he struck a strong blow against idolatry. In order to preserve the independence of his Christian spirituality, he refused to bow to any object, even the Imperial Rescript on Education. Of course there are various ways of looking at this issue. One might say that to refuse to show respect to something that is revered by the rest of the Japanese people simply because he was a Christian was in fact a expression of formalism in itself. It might also be said that spiritual freedom is something that is all right to adhere to in private, but in public one should conform to widely accepted social practice. However, I see Uchimura's stand against idolatry as being equivalent to that made by Elijah against Baalism.

Third, I think he provided us with a new direction in regard to the relationship between race and religion. When he first arrived in Sapporo to enter the Sapporo Agricultural College, he was very unhappy with the prevalence of Christianity, even going so far as to pray at the Sapporo Shinto Shrine saying, "Please drive out this odious false religion from the land of the gods." However, as soon as he awoke to Christianity, he became determined to devote his life to the "Two J's," Jesus and Japan. The epitaph on his grave reads:

I for Japan,
Japan for the world,
The world for Christ,
And all for God.

I think that this speaks eloquently of his spiritual development, resolving his inner conflicts, between Christian faith and ideas about the mission of the country and the world, into a higher unity.

Fourth, Kanzo Uchimura struggled long and hard for social justice. This can be seen from his anti-war stance during the Russo-Japanese War (1904–5), his vehement criticism of the Ashio copper mine that was responsible for polluting the surrounding area, and for his joining with Ruiko Kuroiwa and Shusui Kotoku to form the Idealism Organization.

Of course, Kanzo Uchimura had several shortcomings in his personality. While his uncompromising spirit of independence would have made him a man of steel as one of Jesus' envoys, it failed to make him a man of great success. He was always haunted by feelings of independence, freedom, and solitude. His tendency to glorify Christian martyrdom was one of the reasons why his life was marked by so much unhappiness.

Kanzo Uchimura was actually a reincarnation of the Old Testament prophet Jeremiah, while his disciple Tadao Yanaibara was a reincarnation of St. Peter. Both were high spirits, charged with spreading Christianity in Japan.

If I may add a word about Uchimura's limitations; his Non-church Christianity was not a denial of the Church as such, but represented a meeting of people without a set church. However, his stress of the word "Non-church" became a hindrance to the organizational development of his teachings.

9. Masaharu Taniguchi's "Truth of Life" Philosophy

Masaharu Taniguchi was born in Karasuhara village, Kobe, on November 22, 1893 and he lived until the ripe old age of ninety-two before dying in June 1985. In his youth, he was a follower of Onisaburo Deguchi (1871–1948), who co-founded the new religion, called Omoto-kyo (Great Origin). The Omoto-kyo preached that it was not long until the Last Judgment Day when all humankind would be punished by God for its sins, but Taniguchi felt that this position was too extreme for him to follow and so he left.

Later, Japan was to suffer from a rain of fire and was defeated in World War II, just as Onisaburo Deguchi had prophesied, but the young Taniguchi could not believe that God would choose to punish people in this way. The God he believed in was a God of love. Nothing would convince him that the Father in heaven would want to punish His children in this way. Sickness and disaster strike both the individual as well as the group, but this is actually the effect of thoughts that run contrary to the Truth, not a form of divine punishment. However, Taniguchi had yet to awaken to this principle.

After many trials and errors, he finally attained enlightenment by receiving a revelation from a high spirit. His enlightenment can be summed up in the following:

1. The true meaning of the Buddhist saying "Matter is void, void is matter," is that this world and the other world, the soul and the body, should not be thought of as a duality; there is only the monistic Truth.

2. Therefore, the objects and phenomena of this world are no more than shadows of the "Images of Truth," which are one with God and both are pure light.

Consequently, there is no such thing as the physical body or its disease.

3. Therefore, people of this world should live, carrying in them the light that is the true source of all life. The true way to live is to manifest the divinity that exists within us as children of God.

This was the central core of Taniguchi's enlightenment and his philosophy of light was based on this monism. He proclaimed that all religions, be they Christianity, Buddhism or Shinto, stemmed from a single God and were simply different facets of a single teaching, and adopted a tolerant attitude that embraced them all. In this spirit, he headed the religious movement known as "Seicho-no-Ie" (House of Growth) for a period of fifty-five years.

The first characteristic of this movement was that it was the first to adopt the American New Thought religion[1] (which Taniguchi had introduced to Japan and incorporated into his own particular philosophy), making the resulting creed very instructive. Its second characteristic was that it utilized numerous psychological techniques, a revolutionary notion unprecedented in religions up to that time. The third characteristic was that the movement took advantage of the printing press to spread Taniguchi's message through the publication of numerous books.

---

1. New Thought originated in the United States in the 19th century. New Thought stresses the power of the mind which is believed to be able to overcome various problems such as illness, and improve everyday life.

However, leaving aside his message that all religions were one, if we look at his work up to the time of his death, it is evident that it represents an attempt to revive the teachings of the Shinto gods, and was a reformation of Japanese Shinto brought about through the incorporation of foreign religions and philosophies. In other words, the revival movement of Shinto that had been started by the Kurozumi-kyo, Konko-kyo, Tenri-kyo and Omoto-kyo was developed and brought to completion through Taniguchi's Seicho-no-Ie movement.

He never knew who his guiding spirit was while he was in this world, simply referring to it as the great god of Seicho-no-Ie and telling his followers that it was Sumiyoshi-no-Okami or the Kanzeon Bodhisattva. He never realized that it was in fact Ame-no-Minakanushi-no-Kami (Mikoto), the principle god in the Japanese pantheon. Masaharu Taniguchi's main written work, *The Truth of Life*, consists of forty volumes, all of which were created through automatic writing when his body was under the control of Ame-no-Minakanushi-no-Kami or his attendant spirits.

It goes without saying that the core principle of Shinto is the monism of light. This states that this world is not a confrontation of Light and Darkness, but simply that the Light falls on some places and not on others. There is originally no darkness and if a light is lit, darkness will disappear. A deep love runs through this philosophy that strives to spread the light over the Earth. However, people who do not fully understand this philosophy will shut their eyes to the difference between good and evil and therefore it can be said to have both its merits and demerits.

It cannot be said that Ame-no-Minakanushi-no-Kami's philosophy represents the consensus of the heavenly realm or that it was capable of saving all humankind. I do not think Mr. Taniguchi pays enough attention to the fact that the ability to distinguish between good and evil is the beginning of wisdom. Also, I find that his teachings lack the idea of breaking away from hell, which is the initial step for salvation, nor do they provide any convincing explanation as to how evil spirits haunt people. Masaharu Taniguchi was Izanagi-no-Mikoto in a previous incarnation in Japan, but after that he lived as the European philosopher Plotinus, which explains the strong philosophical leaning in his teachings.

10. The Right Law Teachings of Shinji Takahashi

Even more recently, we find Shinji Takahashi, who was born in Nagano Prefecture in 1927 and died in 1976. However, he did not begin to preach until the last seven or eight years of his life. His message spread rapidly and his organization, God Light Association (GLA), grew with remarkable speed, but unfortunately he died of overwork at the age of forty-eight when he was still in his prime, and the movement lost its momentum. After his death, he was succeeded by his daughter, who was still only nineteen years old. This caused a certain amount of upset within the movement and his message lost its vigor.

Shinji Takahashi's aim was to create a Buddhist revival, but he did not attain an understanding of the core concepts of Buddhism and never got beyond the level of the yogi asceticism that Shakyamuni had undergone before attaining enlightenment. Takahashi tended to believe that "enlightenment equals spiritual power," and he never managed to understand that "wisdom," "faith" and "spreading of Buddha's words" were the vital characteristics of Buddhism.

However, whereas Masaharu Taniguchi preached a message based mainly on Shinto tradition, which also contained elements of Buddhism, Christianity and New Thought, Shinji Takahashi emphasized the revival of Buddhism, while explaining that Christianity, Judaism and Islam all shared the same roots. For this stance he deserves recognition.

If we look at the central pillars of Takahashi's teachings, we see that first, although he was rather lacking in theory, his teaching was based around Shakyamuni's Noble Eightfold Path, placing a lot of importance on self-reflection. In other words, the true significance of self-reflection is that it clears the clouds of negative thoughts from the mind and allows the Light of Buddha to shine in, thus facilitating communication with one's guardian and guiding spirits.

His second point was that one should avoid extremes of the left or right and enter the Middle Way, as this is the only way to realize great harmony.

The third point was to emphasize that the main reason for spiritual training is to correct one's "thoughts and deeds."

The fourth point was to make it clear that in the same way that people are born in various eras and geographical locations through reincarnation, the True Law has also undergone various transitions. In addition to this, Takahashi demonstrated, through spiritual phenomenon, that people were able to remember the languages they had spoken in previous incarnations, thus proving that they had lived in India, China, or Israel in the past. However, it must be realized that many cases were faked by his personal family or disciples, so the results were not always reliable.

The fifth and final point is that through his investigation into the mind, he was able to demonstrate the relationship between the mechanism of the mind and the laws of physics.

These were the main features of his teachings, but now I would like to think about his reason for being born and his mission on Earth as looked at from the Real World. The core spirit of Shinji Takahashi's life form is called Enlil, a being from the ninth dimension. To be more precise, he is from the Minor Heaven and has a baleful side to his character, which means that if his teachings are taken seriously, it is difficult to say whether good or evil would come of it. Enlil had a strong influence on ancient Judaism and, looking back over the three thousand year history of the

Jewish people, one could say that it was a history of persecution at the hands of a god of vengeance.

Previously incarnated as En-no-gyoja, Takahashi
founded Shugendo (mountain asceticism) in Japan. It is a
little known fact that the true identity of the Ushitora-no-
Konjin god that guided the oppressed Omoto-kyo was none
other than En-no-gyoja and related spirits.

I discussed Shinji Takahashi's merits and demerits at
length in my book *The Laws of the Sun*, but in brief he
deserves to be criticized for pretending to be Buddha when
he was in fact a Sennin (hermit wizard), using negative
spiritual phenomena to attract people's attention and giving
momentum to the occult boom within new religions.

For my part, I believe it is important for people to learn
about their spiritual side in order to break their attachment
to this world. However, I feel I must warn you that this
tendency to place too much emphasis on spiritual or supernatural powers is what has led to the recent spread of
spurious religious organizations like Kiriyama Mikkyo
(Agon-shu), Mahikari Groups, Shin'nyo-en, or Aum Shinri-
kyo, which are a hotbed for the production of evil spirits.
The important thing to remember is that the true purpose of
religion does not lie in casting aside the affairs of this world
and concentrating solely on those of the Real World. You
should realize that the real aim of religion is to search for a
happiness that continues from this world to the next.

To put it simply, the difference between true and false
religions lies in whether the followers have experienced

spiritual development. We need to continue to search for the deep wisdom that exists within Buddhism.

Chapter Six
Flying to the Future

1. 2000–2100 A.D.

In Chapters Two to Five, I presented an outline of the activities of the Guiding Spirits of Light through history. At the same time, I gave a detailed account of the developments in terrestrial history as seen from the Real World. Now, in this final chapter, I would like to offer a glimpse of the events that await humanity in the future. I will not go into too much detail in order to avoid binding people into a set course of events, but I hope I will be able to cast a ray of hope for the people yet to come.

If I wanted, I could give a concrete picture of the things to come, but if I were to do this, it would leave no room for independent action. It is for this reason that prophesies are necessarily couched in abstract terms. If I presented a comprehensive picture of the future, there would be a danger of it becoming a heavy burden on the people and causing them to lose their will to endeavor. Therefore, I intend to gloss over the bad events somewhat and only provide accurate descriptions of the good. I hope that this approach will serve to guide the future generations in a positive direction.

In writing this, I have purposely avoided making any mention of events that will occur between now (1986 when the first Japanese edition was written) and the beginning of the twenty-first century. The reason for this is that some shocking events may await humankind during the next few decades. It will be a period of fear and unease, when people will talk about the end of the world. False religions will spring up in Japan and throughout the world, and people will appear to be selling their souls to the devil. World politics will disintegrate into a myriad of different groups, and at one point the United Nations will cease to operate. Conflict will break out in the Middle East and the feeling of war will permeate the air of the powerful nations.

During this period, messengers of the Truth will begin to appear in places throughout the world, and the sun of the Truth will shine forth from Japan, gradually spreading its light to cover the world. Thus, in the midst of unease, people will see the light of hope. In their fear of death, they will hear voices spreading the gospel. In this way, when things seem at their worst, the greatest good will show its light, a light that will continue to grow.

Between 2020 and 2037 Japan will become to the world what Jerusalem or Mecca is now, and this will be Japan's golden age. Japan will be admired throughout the world as the place where the Truth was first revealed, but eventually the light of Truth will pass southwards.

In 2050s, the light will pass to a man in Bangkok, Thailand. This man will be a reincarnation of the Archangel Gabriel who was once incarnated as Leonardo da Vinci. In around 2080, the spirit of the prophet Elijah will be reincarnated in what is now Jakarta, Indonesia, and he will raise up the Truth on a grand scale.

2. 2100–2200 A.D.

In around 2100, it will become possible for people to experience new worlds. The new trend will be for people to visit outer space; it will not become as common as overseas travel is today, but approximately one in ten will choose to try the experience.

Work will be well underway to construct space stations on the moon, and the five most powerful countries will already have completed theirs. Approximately ten thousand people will decide to migrate there in the hope of creating a new Garden of Eden that will transcend barriers of race and color. There will be three regular round-trip flights between Earth and the moon daily and the journey will take approximately twenty hours each way.

As there is no oxygen on the moon, people will live in transparent, hemispherical domes approximately one kilometer (half a mile) in diameter. These will contain gigantic oxygen production and artificial light generating plants. An interesting thing about the domes is that they will be fitted with an artificial sun, about ten meters (thirty-three feet) in diameter, that will travel along the inside circumference of the dome. It will rise in the east, cross the zenith and sink in the west in an effort by the builders to recreate a terrestrial environment on the moon.

Using my spiritual clairvoyance, I can see underground passageways leading out from the domes to the lunar surface, where numerous mechanical excavators are working. The moon contains numerous energy-producing ores that are not available on Earth and these will be mined to supply power for the colonies. Water will be produced scientifically through the chemical reaction of hydrogen and oxygen; I can see it being collected inside the dome in a reservoir two hundred meters (six hundred and fifty feet) in size.

In the twenty-second century, aeronautical engineering will finally discover the secret of antigravity engines that will make it possible for planes to rise and descend vertically and hover at will. This will be achieved by using the principle of magnetic attraction and repulsion to create a machine that is capable of attracting or repulsing the gravity of a planetary body at will.

Another revolutionary invention of the twenty-second century will be a device that makes it possible to communicate with the spirit world. At present we have to rely on specially gifted psychics to communicate with the spirits who have left this world and returned to the fourth dimension and beyond. In the future a machine will be developed that is capable of picking up spiritual wavelengths and converting them into speech.

Unfortunately, however, it will still be impossible to communicate with the high spirits of the dimensions higher than the fifth dimension; interaction will be limited to the inhabitants of the fourth dimension. This will mean that when the high spirits wish to communicate with the inhabitants of Earth, they will be handicapped by having to do so through an intermediary of the fourth dimension. Another problem is that the people on Earth will be unable to choose a particular spirit with whom to communicate. They will only be able to make contact if someone in the fourth dimension happens to intercept the communication from the Earth and helps them to seek out a particular spirit. Another complication is that many of the inhabitants of hell are not up to date, so they will find it very difficult to understand this method of communication. This will result in a great deal of confusion.

The problem with the development of this machine to communicate with the spirits is that there are too many people prepared to believe unconditionally whatever the spirits tell them and, depending on the character of the spirit they manage to contact, this can cause a lot of unhappiness. For this reason, the mission of the high spirits who become incarnated on Earth in the twenty-second century will be to make appraisal of the spirits who are contacted, to reason with the spirits who have fallen to hell, and to draw up prescriptions on behalf of their relatives on Earth to help those lost spirits ascend to heaven. The type of memorial services that Buddhist priests presently hold for the dead will disappear, except in the case of a few minority religions. The majority of people will receive counseling from religious instructors and communicate with their ancestors several times per year.

Another feature of the twenty-second century that deserves mention is the fact that by this time much of the United States will have sunk beneath the ocean, leaving a narrow peninsula running down the line of the present Rocky Mountains. While I do not want to be too precise about exactly when this will happen, I can tell you that it will start with the western half of the continent, around San Francisco in California. This will be followed by the eastern half of the country centered on New York, then finally the Mississippi plain will be the third section to sink. However, this is not a definite prophecy; depending on the self-help and effort of the inhabitants, there is still a chance that it might be prevented.

3. 2200–2300 A.D.

This will be a period of trial for humankind. Life on Earth will have lost its attraction, there will be nothing new and civilization will become stagnant. Gradually signs of decadence will appear among the people. Mechanization will have advanced to such a degree that primary industry will be left almost completely in the hands of robots, and secondary industry and mining will also rely to a large degree on them.

Only commerce and services will still be in the hands of human beings, but machines will have rendered clerical work so minimal that people will only have to deal with negotiations, decision making and planning.

The working day will be approximately four hours, and people will be able to decide whether they want to work mornings or afternoons. They will only work for four days a week and what to do during their spare time will become a major problem. Of course, there will be some people who choose to devote their time to developing themselves spiritually, but the majority will be content to travel down the road to depravity, and their numbers will continue to grow.

To give some examples of the kind of depravity I am talking of, some people will abandon themselves to sexual pleasure, as they have throughout history. Others will think up new games or sports, and devote themselves entirely to them. Still others will use genetic engineering to create new types of plant or animal life. There will be those who build robots for organized fights and gamble on the results, while some will devote themselves to developing supernatural powers, particularly psycho-kinesis.

Due to this tendency toward depravity, a Great Guiding Spirit will be sent down from the ninth dimension of the heavenly realm in order to purify the Earth. The spirit in question will be the Great Guiding Spirit of Light who previously preached in China as Confucius, and he will begin to teach the Law in approximately 2260. His reincarnation is planned to occur in Australia, where the population will have grown to about one hundred million.

In the period 2000 to 2100 the most important area of the world will be Japan, from 2100 to 2200 it will be South-East Asia, then from 2200 to 2300 it will be Australia. This is where Confucius will be reborn and his teachings will continue to focus on human perfection both in terms of character and morality, a subject that has always been dear to his heart. His central theme will be that of the creation of a divine human, the principle of human reformation, and he will use the scholastic approach that served him so well in his last incarnation. However, his teachings will be completely original and will represent a new moral principle.

The central points of Confucius' new philosophy are threefold: first, he states that the basic characteristic of humans is their desire to better themselves, and it is for this reason that they like to study. Second, he says a desire for order is a basic characteristic of human society and that people should be esteemed for the degree of inherent spirituality they manifest. Third, he stresses the principle of improving rivalry through mutual effort, and he teaches that this is the way to personal enlightenment. Those are the main points of his teaching, so when a man appears in Australia in approximately 2260 preaching these principles, you can be sure that he is a reincarnation of Confucius.

Another event that will take place during the twenty-third century will be a movement in the Earth's crust in what was once the USSR. The western half of the country, centered around St. Petersburg, will subside, to be followed by a similar collapse in Central Asia. The Earth will crack and the waters of the Arctic Ocean will rush in to create a new sea in the center of the Eurasian Continent that will be approximately the same size as the present-day Mediterranean.

Volcanoes in South-East Asia will become very active from the twenty-first century. This will lead to a new age of mountain formation that, by the twenty-third century, will be recognizable as the formation of a new continent. This will be the harbinger of the return of the continent of Mu, which used to exist in the southern Pacific. The new continent will be centered on present-day Jakarta in Indonesia. It will begin with the appearance of a large island some time between the year 2000 and 2100. This will be followed by a period of intense mountain formation after 2100. By the twenty-third century the basic shape of the continent will be quite clear although it will take a further one hundred to two hundred years before it is completed. It will be quite a large continent and before long it will become covered with trees and other plant life. The Izu peninsula in Japan will be connected to this new continent, as will Australia, and a large number of people will leave South-East Asia to go and live on it.

4. 2300–2400 A.D.

The beginning of the twenty-fourth century will be marked by violent movements in the Earth's crust and most remarkable of all will be the appearance of a new continent in the Atlantic ocean. This will be caused by a reaction to the sinking of much of what we know of as the United States.

The new continent will rise in the vicinity of the Bermuda Triangle, the same area that Atlantis occupied ten thousand years ago. America—the modern Atlantis—will sink, to be replaced by the original Atlantis. This new continent of Atlantis will not be a separate continent, but will be connected to Canada, creating a long continent that will run north-west to south-east. The newly risen land will be the equivalent of approximately two-thirds of the total area of Canada.

Soon after this new continent appears, the Canadians will begin to move there to live, followed closely by a large number of Europeans seeking a new world. As a result, the new continent will thrive in the second half of the twenty-fourth century; in many ways this period will resemble the era when the Puritans sailed to America to break new ground.

In the latter half of the twenty-fourth century, Martin Luther will be reincarnated in this land to usher in a new religious movement. His main task will be the translation, propagation and dissemination of the Law of El Cantare that I have been preaching. He will start off as a Japanese language teacher in school, but one day he will come across the books I am writing on the Truth as well as various books of spiritual messages from the high spirits, and will devour their contents eagerly. My books on the Truth alone will count in the hundreds and as he delves into this vast trove of knowledge, this Japanese professor will gradually awaken to his own mission. Christianity will still be the dominant religion in the new Atlantis at this time, but due to Martin Luther's efforts, the Truth that we are spreading from the second half of the twentieth century will gradually gain a large following.

However, the heavenly realm will not delegate this job to Martin Luther alone. He will be followed shortly by another great religious reformer, Nichiren. While Martin Luther will spread his message from an academic stand-point, the reincarnated Nichiren will concentrate intensely on "humanity." He will say that there can be no Truth without human beings and no religion without inquiry into humanity.

He will advocate an Eastern philosophy while living in the West. The core of this teaching will be an analysis of the workings of the mind. In other words, he will provide various explanations of how to attain correct states of the mind and stress the importance of practicing them. The correct state of the mind, or Right Mind, is not something that should be hidden within; it is only through outward expression that the kingdom of heaven can be achieved on Earth. He will adopt the motto "True knowledge speaks, true knowledge acts," and develop a powerful creed.

One more famous man of the past will be reincarnated during this period and that is Mohammed, the founder of Islam. In this life too, he will undergo a revelation and begin to communicate with heaven. As before, it will be the Archangel Gabriel who transmits the messages to him, while the ninth dimensional being, Zoroaster, will act as his main guiding spirit. The reincarnated Mohammed's message will deal mainly with the dualism of good and evil, a philosophy that will strike a chord with the people living in that period and spread rapidly.

However, there will be one problem. The spiritual messages that Mohammed will pass on to the people will differ in terms of their content and spirit from those that I, Ryuho Okawa, have been conveying to the world since the second half of the twentieth century. There will be suspicions voiced among certain religious people who adhere blindly to my teachings that Mohammed's messages do not in fact spring from the holy spirits, and this will result in him suffering from religious persecution. For this reason, I would like to take this opportunity to offer him some advice: "Do not be daunted, but at the same time, bear in mind that your message of the duality of good and evil is not the only Truth."

5. 2400–2500 A.D.

In the beginning of the twenty-fifth century yet another great light will be incarnated on Earth. This will be the reincarnation of Jesus Christ. His coming will have been foretold by the reincarnated forms of Nichiren and Mohammed so the people will have been looking forward to his appearance since the latter half of the twenty-fourth century. Word of his impending birth will be passed from mouth to mouth, heart to heart, and, eventually, he will return after a period of twenty-four hundred years to fill the Earth with light.

It is impossible to say just exactly when Jesus will be born, but it is likely to be some time around 2400, and the place scheduled for his advent will be the new continent of Atlantis that is joined to present-day Canada. In this land he will begin to preach a message of Truth that will be relevant to the space age. It will essentially be the same message of love preached by Jesus of Nazareth, but spatially on a much grander scale.

By this time, interaction with extraterrestrials will occur on a regular basis but will give rise to a certain degree of friction due to differences in thought processes between the different races. Already, since the latter half of the 1980s, Earth has been visited regularly by more than ten races of extraterrestrials, but they have yet to enter into open communication with us and are still making preliminary surveys.

The inhabitants of Earth came originally from a variety of different planetary spirit groups, but during hundreds of millions of years of reincarnation, they have surpassed their differences to become an integrated race of Earth dwellers. They have worked together to create a common terrestrial personality while the Great Guiding Spirits of Light have taken turns to come down to Earth through the ages to preach the various phases of the Truth. This has resulted in the development of a spiritual foundation that is shared by all the races. In other words, by being once incarnated as a Buddhist, then as a Christian and then as a Muslim, for example, the people of Earth have created a spiritual base that is common to all of humankind.

However, the time is coming when the human race approaches perfection in their spiritual training, in other words, there will be less and less left to learn from life on Earth. As that happens, the older spirits will travel to other, more advanced worlds to live. On the other hand, those who move out will be replaced by other spirits who will come to Earth to begin their training here.

The arrival of more than ten races of extraterrestrial beings on Earth at present will have very much the same effect as the arrival of the American fleet off the coast of Japan did in the nineteenth century. It will mean the years of isolation are drawing to an end and a new age is approaching. People will still continue to improve themselves through their life on Earth, at least until the thirtieth century, but after that, the older, more advanced spirits will leave this planet to look for a new home.

The period when Jesus is reborn on Earth in the twenty-fifth century will be something of a transitional period. Space travel and emigration to the planets will become much more common, while at the same time the inhabitants of other planets will become regular visitors to Earth, where they will interact with terrestrials. Unfortunately, however, the aliens' concept of the Truth will vary from that of the terrestrials, and this will result in confusion among those on Earth. Differences in lifestyle and behavior will be bad enough, but it will be the disparity in morals that will cause the most damage.

For instance, one race of aliens may believe that food is something provided through heavenly magnanimity, free of charge, and that therefore it is only natural to help themselves to whatever is needed. If they were hungry, they would think they are free to take the nearest plants or fish and eat their fill. On the other hand, they would believe that because machines are made by people and therefore obviously belong to somebody, they should not be taken without permission of the owner.

However, from an earthling's point of view, the aliens' habit of helping themselves to food whenever they feel like it is simple robbery and, no matter what is said, aliens and terrestrials will never be able to understand each other fully, their values being in total opposition to each other.

Another race of extraterrestrials may feel that children are a mutual asset of society, and that public organization should be responsible for their upbringing. Therefore, they would feel that it is wrong for each family to live in a separate house and raise their children as they see fit. Also, while they may find it quite acceptable for a man and woman to live together for a period during their twenties for the express purpose of procreation, they may feel that to do so at any other time would be mere selfishness and something that would not be countenanced by society. It goes without saying that this will also lead to conflict with terrestrial social values.

It will be at a time when society is in turmoil due to these differences that Jesus will be reincarnated on Earth. His message of love will go beyond differences between Earth's people and the extraterrestrial races as he teaches of the marvelous harmony that we all share as children of Buddha. He will tell the people that although they may think of themselves as native to the planet Earth, they are in fact descendants of people from a multitude of planets.

6. 2500–2600 A.D.

The twenty-sixth century sees another period of major seismic activities in the Earth's crust, beginning with the disappearance beneath the ocean of a large portion of the present-day Middle East and southern Africa. War has been going on in the Middle East almost without a break for several hundred years and the resulting clouds of dark, negative thoughts have built up to such an extent that the Light of Buddha is cut off, and the Earth reacts to this by causing the whole area to sink. The same thing happened in the final days of Atlantis. Once the Light of Buddha is cut off, the resulting disharmonious spiritual energy creates movements in the Earth's crust.

Let me explain the mechanics behind the destruction of these continents. As I stated in my book *The Laws of the*

Sun, numerous civilizations in the past have disappeared when the continents that housed them sank beneath the ocean in a matter of a few days. The reason for this is always the same. People's unharmonious thoughts create dark clouds of negative energy that cuts off the Light of Buddha and the Earth reacts to this by causing the tectonic plates to move. But how does this happen?

The important thing to remember when considering this kind of event is that the Earth is not just a gigantic mass of matter. The Earth is itself a gigantic life form, although from the viewpoint of the Grand Cosmos even the planet is little more than a single molecule. The Earth is an independent life form, and as such its body is in a state of constant flux like any other living thing. The flowing magma in its depths is its blood, the water in the seas its bodily fluid, and the formation of mountains and subsidence of land all part of its metabolism.

From the point of view of the Earth as a living being, areas that are inhabited by people who have sold their souls to the devil are the equivalent of areas that have been infected by viruses. Therefore, its first priority is to disinfect the area and destroy the viruses. When a scab forms on the body of either man or animal, they will scratch at it until it has been removed; in the same way, the Earth uses its powers of self-purification to try and eliminate areas of disharmony. This cannot honestly be described as a form of heavenly punishment; it is merely the natural life-support function of the planet as a life form.

In contrast to the sinking of the Middle East and southern Africa, a new continent will rise from the Indian Ocean halfway between the Indian subcontinent and Africa. This is the area where the Lamudian continent used to exist and so let us tentatively refer to it as the New Lamudian continent.

When it first appears, it will be approximately ten times the area of Japan, but gradually it will spread until it is connected with the northern part of the African continent. Its appearance will resemble that of a rope that is suddenly lifted out of water from one end, causing numerous islands to form where it breaks the surface, then gradually the areas in between are filled in until it becomes a single land. The movement will become most pronounced in the second half of the twenty-sixth century.

By the time New Lamudia has joined with the northern part of Africa to create a new land mass that resembles that of the ancient continent of Garna, the central and southern area of Africa will already have sunk beneath the ocean.

Present-day Europe will also have undergone some drastic changes. Some areas will have started to sink at around the beginning of the twenty-second century, and during the twenty-third century yet another region will disappear. Using my spiritual vision to obtain a view of the whole of Europe in the latter half of the twenty-sixth century, I find that dramatic changes have taken place:

The British Isles remain unchanged, but both Spain and Portugal have disappeared without a trace while the Mediterranean Sea has spread to cover much of southern

France. Germany will be unscathed, but parts of Eastern Europe will have disappeared, triggered by the great subsidence that occurred around St. Petersburg in the twenty-third century. Norway and Finland will still remain more or less the same.

Greece and Italy will have disappeared and people will talk of them as being mythical countries that used to exist in the Mediterranean Sea, much as today we discuss Atlantis or Mu. When we talk of the philosophers Socrates, Plato or Aristotle, we think of them as having been living, breathing people, but two or three hundred years after Greece disappears beneath the waves, they will have been transformed into gods who lived in some mythical country.

At the end of the twenty-sixth century the prosperity of present-day Japan will be talked of in the same way as people now talk about the riches of Greece or Rome. Japan's prosperity reaches its peak by the year 2100 and after this period its national power will go into rapid decline. A leading culture is created by large numbers of high spirits gathering in a particular area at a particular time. If we bear this fact in mind, you may realize that at the end of the twenty-sixth century, the high spirits will be gathering in an area of the world other than Japan.

7. 2600–2700 A.D.

The twenty-seventh century will see a lull in the movements of the Earth's crust after the violent changes described in the preceding section. Also, at the beginning of this century, Koot Hoomi, an inhabitant of the ninth dimension, will be incarnated on New Lamudia, the continent that rose up from the depths of the Indian Ocean. He appeared on Earth before as the Greek Archimedes (287–212 B.C.) then as Newton (1643–1727), and it is easy to see from this that this soul excels in all areas of scientific study. The Light of Buddha is divided into seven colors—yellow, white, red, blue, green, violet, and silver—and Newton is the leader of the silver rays.

Before I go any further, I think that an explanation of the properties of the different colors would be in order and they are as follows:

First, there is yellow, although its actual hue is closer to gold. This color is controlled by Shakyamuni Buddha and is the color of Truth and the Law itself. The yellow light shines down from Shakyamuni in the ninth dimension, through the eighth and seventh and as far as the sixth dimension and below. Among the members of this group are the Buddhist spirits. I named this book *The Golden Laws* as this is just another way of saying "The teaching of Shakyamuni Buddha."

The white light rays are governed by Jesus Christ in the ninth dimension. White is the color of love, and it is for this reason that doctors and nurses, who embody the light of love, wear white clothes. The souls who are followers of Jesus Christ are often referred to as the "White Brotherhood," and their existence has become well known in recent years through the work of numerous psychics.

Next, we come to the red rays that are governed by Moses in the ninth dimension. Red stands for leadership and it has a strong influence over politics and military affairs.

The fourth color is blue, which controls ideas and abstract thoughts. The ninth dimensional being who has been given control over this is Zeus. He not only gives guidance in the fields of literature and the arts, but is also concerned with philosophy. I must point out, however, that in the case of Socrates or Plato, whose philosophies dealt with the Truth itself, Shakyamuni also offered guidance.

The fifth color is green and is the domain of Manu, a Tathagata of the ninth dimension. Green controls nature, the environment and great harmony. Lao-tzu and Chuang-tzu, whose philosophies focused on harmony with nature, were strongly influenced by the green part of the spectrum that governs harmony.

The sixth color is violet and controls order, customs, ceremony and morals. This color is under the control of the great Chinese philosopher Confucius, and the spirits of the Japanese Shinto religion are within a branch of this color.

The seventh color, silver, is the color of science, and controls physics, medicine, mathematics, chemistry. Albert Einstein, Hideki Yukawa and the other great scientists of the world were all influenced by this silvery-white color. As I mentioned at the beginning of this section, this color is in the charge of Isaac Newton, one of the Tathagata of the ninth dimension.

This covers seven of the great Divine Spirits of the ninth dimension with human character, but there are three others who are not directly in charge of one of the seven colors of the spectrum but act as regulators.

First of these is Enlil, whose task is to channel the fierceness and destructive energy of the gods into creation, and to raise spiritual awareness. The second is Maitreya, who strives to transform compassion into concrete acts. Third and last there is Zoroaster, also known as Zarathustra, who, after he founded Zoroastrianism in Persia, was reincarnated as Mani and went on to found Manichaeism. His role is to adjust people's understanding of good and evil to match the period in which they live. He is responsible for deciding just what should be considered good and what evil at different periods of history.

The above is a rough guide to the ten great Divine Spirits who dwell in the ninth dimension and their particular duties. Isaac Newton is one of these, and when he is reincarnated on Earth in the twenty-seventh century he will focus his energies on creating a scientific civilization appropriate to the space age. During this period he will probably invent a spaceship that is capable of moving through the fourth dimension and above, enabling people to travel to any star in the universe, irrespective of distance.

8. 2700–2800 A.D.

The continent that will be in supremacy at this time is the one that appeared in the Indian Ocean and which we can call New Lamudia or New Garna. I would like now to describe something of the civilization that will exist there.

The most obvious characteristic to meet the eye is that the continent is divided into three different colored regions. The eastern third of the continent is devoted mainly to industry, with factories and production plants accounting for most of the land space. This dense concentration of factory buildings creates the impression that the land is covered with white tiles.

The central part is principally given over to residential space. Looked at from above it can be seen that the basic color of the buildings is orange and in the center of this orange expanse is a circular area about one hundred kilometers (sixty-two miles) in diameter that holds the office district. The government and corporate buildings are densely packed into this circular plot and radiating from it is the residential area, which has been divided into eight sections reflecting the various occupations or religions of the inhabitants. This means that people live in groups with those who share their interests or beliefs.

The western third of the continent is green. It is devoted to agriculture and filled with orchards, fields and dairy farms for as far as the eye can see. Holiday villas can be seen dotting the hills to the north while the southern coast boasts a resort town. If you look carefully into the waters even further south, you should just be able to see the outline of the underwater city that exists there. It consists of numerous transparent hemispherical domes that dot the continental shelf from a depth of about fifty meters to one hundred meters (One hundred and sixty-five to three hundred and thirty feet). These domes are connected with the outside world by a train system that passes through a network of undersea tunnels. This city was not constructed to provide homes for the people so much as to facilitate oceanographic studies and the creation of fish farms.

Among the research undertaken is the exploration and mining of the mineral resources that exist beneath the ocean floor as well as experiments in the extraction of gold and uranium from sea water. I can see the sea water being filtered to create drinking water or broken down into oxygen and hydrogen, with the oxygen being piped to the domes for their occupants to breathe while the hydrogen is solidified and used as fuel.

Small submarines go out from the domes to dig into the seabed with mechanical arms. Once a sufficient area has been prepared in this way, the rocks are sucked in through hoses and pass through machines that automatically separate precious and useful minerals. The area around the underwater city also contains large oil stocks; numerous submarines go out and use robots to drill for oil. Since all the oil fields on land have been long since exhausted, there is no alternative but to develop new resources on the continental shelf. The crude oil is refined in the underwater city, then fed to the mammoth industrial area on the ground through an underwater pipeline.

Another activity of the underwater city is the management of fish farms. Numerous varieties of fish are raised in these but the fish are not confined within particular areas; instead, they are allowed to swim free. Columns about ten meters (thirty-three feet) in height can be seen dotting the ocean floor, and at the top of these are honeycomb-like structures that provide places for the fish to live. In between these pillars is an empty space where food is provided automatically three times a day. When the food is provided, a particular tune is played, each tune corresponding to the food that is preferred by a certain species of fish. In this way, it is possible to train the different species of fish to react to a certain piece of music and teach them to gather in the open space when it is played, making it possible to catch a whole school of fish in a single net. These events are monitored by underwater cameras, allowing the workers in the control room to oversee the breeding and catching of the fish from within the city.

These fish farms are a popular source of employment among young people because they entail the use of advanced technology. It goes without saying that in addition to fish, seaweed is also grown for human consumption at the underwater cities.

9. 2800–2900 A.D.

Another epochal change will take place during the twenty-ninth century. This will take the form of a great reformation of the Truth. During the early years of this century one of the Great Guiding Spirits of Light will come down to Earth. He will be a reincarnation of the spirit who was once born in Egypt under the name of Moses, and he will appear in the New Lamudian continent.

He will be a different man from the one who led the Hebrews out of Egypt. In those days he was a political leader, a miracle worker and a man with superior spiritual powers. When he appears next, he will represent a completely new kind of leader. His teachings will obviously center around spirituality, but this time he will also exhibit supernatural abilities extensively.

By this time, space travel via the fourth dimension will have reached the stage of practical application and this will result in a change in the conditions of the people who travel in this way. Until this time, the third dimension and the spirit world of the fourth dimension and above were strictly separate. However, if a person hopes to travel through the fourth dimension en route to a distant star, he cannot very well keep his three-dimensional physical body as it is when he goes.

When I was explaining the Physics of the Light of Buddha in Chapter One of this book, I stated that the existence of objects in the third dimension is governed by vibrations of a certain wavelength. In other words, objects that exist in the fourth dimension have fourth-dimensional vibrations whereas objects that exist in the third dimension have slightly cruder vibrations that limit them to this world. Therefore, in order to allow a spaceship to travel through the fourth dimension, it would be necessary to create an apparatus that would alter its vibrations to that of the fourth dimension.

However, human beings are not machines; they are controlled by a spiritual consciousness. When the vibrations of the body are altered to the fourth-dimensional frequency, that is to say when they have been broken down in a three-dimensional sense and become invisible, it destroys the harmony between the body and the soul, which is originally from the fourth dimension or above. Therefore, special training is required for the soul to control the fragmented parts after the human body has been broken down into fourth-dimensional elements. This will create a demand for a leader capable of teaching people to train the mind to undergo such a situation. The reincarnated Moses will take this role. He will be born with the ability to transport himself through teleportation, but in order for him to use this skill, he will have to understand thoroughly the Laws that govern the Real World that stretches over the fourth dimension and above.

If teleportation is practiced without this knowledge, it will lead to schizophrenia. This is because the soul will lose its ability to control its physical body, creating a distortion in the silver cord that joins them both together. Therefore, in the twenty-ninth century, the Guiding Spirits of Light will teach those who are capable of transporting themselves instantly from one place to another through teleportation the rules that govern the harmony between the soul and the body. The Guiding Spirits of Light will warn against the dangers of becoming enamored of cults that worship supernatural abilities, and they will teach people about the truthful life that humans should live. Just because they may be able to travel through the fourth dimension does not mean that they are superior to others or that they have attained enlightenment. There are worlds in the fifth dimension and beyond that contain people who are infinitely more enlightened. This is the message that they will patiently teach.

It is very dangerous for people with psychic skills to turn aside in the quest for supernatural powers. In this age, there will be numerous people who are capable of teleportation or telepathy and it is very difficult to teach them the message of love and compassion. The reincarnated Moses will also have to teach the people the true meaning of justice, as the supernatural powers will become a threat to the people living on Earth in many different ways.

10. 2900–3000 A.D. and Beyond

As the world moves into the thirtieth century, science and technology will reach their peak on Earth. First let me tell you what I have seen there. There are two main centers of civilization on Earth during this period—New Atlantis in the Atlantic Ocean and New Lamudia in the Indian Ocean. With regard to religion, the inhabitants of New Atlantis will still believe in the teachings of the soul, but in New Lamudia they will have become enamored with the worship of the supernatural.

If we look at the civilization of New Atlantis from above, we can see a city radiating out from the space communication base in the center. The development of pyramid power will be at its height at this time, and I can see numerous pyramid-shaped buildings made out of reinforced glass standing in rows. As well as absorbing the sun's rays, these buildings also absorb the cosmic rays that are used as a new source of power. The outer surface of the reinforced glass buildings shine with a spectrum of seven colors, like a rainbow that changes continually through the course of the day. During the night, the space terminus is so brightly lit that it resembles daytime—it is truly an amazing sight.

Another characteristic of this period is the large number of magnetic walkways linking the various buildings. They actually look like rainbow bridges hanging in the air, one to two hundred meters (three hundred and twenty-five to six hundred and fifty feet) above the ground and shining with an orange or yellow light.

Although I call them walkways, this is a rather misleading name. They are in fact magnetic force fields that repel the natural magnetic field generated by human bodies so that, when people stand on the walkway, they in fact hover about five centimeters (two inches) above it. They then take a control box from their pocket and, pressing the forward button, glide effortlessly along the walkway as if they were standing on a conveyor belt, until they press the stop button and come to an immediate halt. People from the twentieth century would be amazed if they could see this transport system of the thirtieth century.

H. G. Wells wrote of a time machine at the end of the nineteenth century, and during the thirtieth century the science of the New Atlantean civilization will have brought his dream into a reality. The principle behind this invention is that if a machine could be created that would travel faster than light, it would be able to break through the wall of the present time, which stands between the past and the future.

The machine will actually be developed in the beginning of the thirtieth century, but the crew who board it disappear somewhere into the past or future, resulting in a great deal of confusion. A second expedition will be sent out on a rescue mission, followed by a third expedition, but all of them disappear, creating a serious social problem. Nobody will know when in time and where they are, and there will be no way of searching for them. However, the great psychics of the period will eventually enlist the help of the spirits in heaven and eventually some of the time travelers will be located and rescued.

The appearance of the time travelers is recorded in history, for example, in the story of the Tengu (a long-nosed spirit) who appeared on Mt. Kurama in Japan in the seventh century. Some pictures on the walls of the pyramids in Egypt were in fact depictions of men from the future. Time travelers also appeared on the Nazca plain in South America, where the ancient Incans mistook them for gods. The four-legged vehicle that is mentioned by Ezekiel in the

Old Testament is not a UFO, as some would like to believe, but was a time machine from the thirtieth century.

In the end, only thirty people will take part in the time travel project before it is banned by the government due to a strong anti-time travel lobby. By this time, H. G. Wells will be considered a prophet by the people. In this way the thirtieth century will become a century of science, but this trend will not last. From the thirty-first century, scientific civilization will start a period of long decline.

Also during this period, spiritually advanced New Atlanteans will migrate to other planets in large numbers to build a new utopia. In the same way that people originally came from numerous stars to struggle and persevere to build a utopia here on Earth, their descendants will make a similar journey to find a place where they can develop and refine the soul. The first wave of emigration will occur in the thirty-first century, to be followed by another mass exodus in the thirty-fifth century.

The human race will continue to live on Earth for another hundred million years and during that time they will witness the rise and fall of innumerable civilizations. However, no two civilizations will ever be quite the same, and it is this fact that will allow people to continue to pursue their spiritual learning for eternity.

After teaching the Law for a period of approximately fifty years, from the late twentieth to early twenty-first century, I will return to the heavenly realm where I shall offer instruction to numerous Guiding Spirits of Light. I will return to Earth again in two thousand eight hundred years time and look forward to meeting many of you again during that life.

Author's Notes

Chapter Three
(Note 1 page 75)
The caste system is an exclusive social structure that places restrictions on every aspect of life, including marriage, eating, and work. People often understand caste as referring to the four different groups mentioned, whereas in India these groupings are referred to as Varna and the true word for caste, referring to the different groups that people are born into, is Jati.

Chapter Four
(Note 2 page 124)
According to Tendai Hongaku Philosophy, human beings are basically enlightened, whereas Shigaku philosophy states that people can only attain enlightenment through spiritual discipline. The former, therefore, represents a corruption of basic Buddhist beliefs.

(Note 3 page 129)

"Ju-jushin"—Treatise on the Ten Stages of the Development of the Mind. An explanation of the stages of enlightenment, based on the Kegon (Garland) Sutra:

1) Isho Teiyo Shin

    The state of an animal. A stage with no goodness, governed by instinct—the level of being involved in the evil deeds of single-minded invocation.

2) Gudo Jisai Shin

    The stage where goodness first sprouts in the mind of a rude child—the level of human teaching.

3) Yodo Mui Shin

    The stage where one awakens to religion like a peaceful child and attains a religious peace of mind—the level of heavenly teaching.

4) Yui-un Muga Shin

    The stage where one realizes that everything is created through the temporary harmonization of the five spiritual and physical elements, but does not question the existence of those elements—the level of self-enlightenment through study.

5) Batsugo Inju Shin

    The stage where one can recognize that the cause of suffering is delusive desires and is willing to remove them—the level of self-enlightenment without guidance.

6) Taen Daijo Shin

The stage where one struggles to save all sentient beings through boundless compassion—the level of the Hosso Sect.

7) Kakushin Fusho Shin

The level of enlightenment where one realizes that one's mind is free from all restraints—the level of the Sanron Sect.

8) Ichido Mui Shin

The stage where one realizes that the ultimate Truth exists in all things in their natural state—the level of the Tendai Sect.

9) Gokumu Jisho Shin

The level of enlightenment where one realizes that creation does not consist of concrete objects but is the manifestation of the Truth—the level of the Kegon Sect.

10) Himitsu Shogon Shin

The ultimate level of enlightenment where one can see through to the essential nature of one's own mind and understand the whole Truth—the level of the Shingon Sect.

(Note 4 page 129)

T'ien-t'ai Chih-i set out the chronological order in which Shakyamuni Buddha explained the five great sutras and used this as a way of ranking them. From the bottom these were as follows:

1) Kegon period—Kegon (Garland) Sutra
2) Rokuon period—Agon (Agama) Sutra
3) Hodo period—Yuima (Vimalakirti-nirdesa) Sutra / Shoman (Srimaladevi-simhanada) Sutra
4) Hannya period—Hannya (Prajina-paramita) Sutra
5) Hokke Nehan period—Hokke (Lotus) Sutra / Nehan (Nirvana) Sutra.

Modern scholars have ascertained that all the main sutras were composed over a period of several centuries after Shakyamuni's death and, therefore, do not attach much significance to this philosophy of "five periods and eight teachings." Despite this, however, we must admire T'ien-t'ai Chih-i for his scholastic analysis of the vast quantity of sutras.

Dimensional Structure of the Real World

Dimension	Name of Realm	Substructure		Development Stage of Love	The Names of the Inhabitants
Ninth	Cosmic Realm (Sun Realm)		Realm of the Sun	God's Love Love of the Saviour	Grand Tathagata, Guru
Eighth	Tathagata Realm (Diamond Realm)	Divine Light Realm Semi-Divine Realm	Realm of Brahma	Existence as love	Tathagata Brahma
Seventh	Bodhisattva Realm			Forgiving love	Bodhisattva
Sixth	Light Realm			Nurturing love	Arhat
Fifth	Realm of the Good			Love for loving (fundamental love)	
Fourth	Posthumous Realm	Astral Realm	Realm of Hell	Instinctive love Love that takes	
Third	The world on earth				

Postscript

The original version of this book was written, together with *The Laws of the Sun*, in 1986, when the author was still only thirty years old, and published the following year. Filled with the sensitivity of youth and exhibiting a bold literary style, it soon won a following of eager readers not only in Japan but throughout the world.

The years that have passed since then have seen the rise of the Institute for Research in Human Happiness (IRH); it has now become a major spiritual movement, enabling me as its leader to achieve a new stage of enlightenment.

This new edition of *The Golden Laws* preserves the framework of the old edition, but has in addition a certain amount of praise for and criticism of the achievements of previous leaders of Light. I felt this task was vital if we are to usher in a prosperous future and not simply remain satisfied with the teachings of the past. In particular, I have added significantly to Chapter Four, "The Land of the Rising Sun," which deals with the work of spiritual leaders in Japan. And in Chapter Five I have gone into more detail concerning the works of Mohammed, as well as adding a critique on the teachings of the Japanese men of religion, Uchimura, Taniguchi, and Takahashi.

In a scholarly sense, this revised edition can be said to be more refined, while in a religious context it exhibits a higher degree of enlightenment. *The Golden Laws* offers a temporal discourse on the Truth. My sincere hope is that, together with *The Laws of the Sun* and *The Laws of Eternity*, the first and third books in my trilogy, it will serve as a useful guide to many people in their spiritual discipline and search for enlightenment.

Ryuho Okawa
July 1995, for the revised Japanese edition

Index of Names

225

WHAT IS IRH?

The Institute for Research in Human Happiness (IRH), Kofuku-no-Kagaku in Japanese, is an organization of people who aim to refine their souls and deepen their wisdom. IRH spreads the light of Truth, with the aim of creating utopia, an ideal world on Earth.

The teachings of IRH are based on the spirit of Buddhism. The two main pillars are the attainment of spiritual wisdom and the practice of love that gives.

Members study Buddha's Truth (the Law) and practice self-reflection daily, based on the Truth they learn. In this way they develop a deeper understanding of life and build qualities of leadership for society, enabling them to contribute to the development of the world.

SELF-DEVELOPMENT PROGRAMS

Video lectures and meditation seminars are held at each branch office. By attending seminars, you will be able to:

- Know the purpose of life.
- Know the true meaning of love.
- Know the Laws of success.

- Learn to understand the workings of your soul.
- Learn the importance of meditation and methods.
- Learn how to maintain peace of mind.
- Learn how to overcome the challenges in life.
- Learn how to create a bright future, and more…

IRH MONTHLY MESSAGES

This features lectures by Ryuho Okawa. Each issue also includes a question and answer session on real life problems with Ryuho Okawa. Anyone is able to subscribe to the IRH Monthly Messages. Back issues are also available upon request.

MEDITATION RETREAT

Educational opportunities are provided for people who wish to seek the path of Truth. The Institute organizes meditation retreats for English speakers in Japan. You will be able to find keys to solve the problems in life and restore peace of mind.

For more information, please contact our branch offices or your local area contact.

THE INSTITUTE FOR RESEARCH
IN HUMAN HAPPINESS
Kofuku-no-Kagaku

Tokyo
1-2-38 Higashi Gotanda
Shinagawa-ku
Tokyo 141–0022
Japan
Tel: 81-3-5793-1729
Fax: 81-3-5793-1739
Email: tokyo@irh-intl.org
www.irhpress.co.jp

New York
2nd Fl. Oak Tree Center
2024 Center Avenue
Fort Lee, NJ 07024
U.S.A.
Tel: 1-201-461-7715
Fax: 1-201-461-7278
Email: ny@irh-intl.org

Los Angeles
Suite 104
3848 Carson Street
Torrance, CA 90503
U.S.A.
Tel: 1-310-543-9887
Fax: 1-310-543-9447
Email: la@irh-intl.org

San Francisco
1291 5th Ave.
Belmont, CA 94002
U.S.A.
Tel / Fax: 1-650-802-9873
Email: sf@irh-intl.org

Hawaii
Suite 19
1259 South Beretania Street
Honolulu, HI 96814
U.S.A.
Tel: 1-808-591-9772
Fax: 1-808-591-9776
Email: hi@irh-intl.org

Toronto
484 Ravineview Way
Oakville, Ontario L6H 6S8
Canada
Tel: 1-905-257-3677
Fax: 1-905-257-2006
Email: toronto@irh-intl.org

London
65 Wentworth Avenue
Finchley, London N3 1YN
United Kingdom
Tel : 44-20-8346-4753
Fax: 44-20-8343-4933
Email: eu@irh-intl.org

Sao Paulo
(Ciencia da Felicidade do
Brasil)
Rua Gandavo
363 Vila Mariana
Sao Paulo, CEP 04023-001
Brazil
Tel: 55-11-5574-0054
Fax: 55-11-5574-8164
Email: sp@irh-intl.org

Seoul
178-6 Songbuk-Dong
Songbuk-ku, Seoul
Korea
Tel: 82-2–762-1384
Fax: 82-2–762-4438
Email: korea@irh-intl.org

Melbourne
P.O.Box 429 Elsternwick
VIC 3185
Australia
Tel / Fax: 61-3-9503-0170
Email: mel@irh-intl.org

OTHER E-MAIL CONTACTS

Florida
Email: florida@irh-intl.org

Albuquerque
Email: abq@irh-intl.org

Boston
Email: boston@irh-intl.org

Chicago
Email: chicago@irh-intl.org

ABOUT THE AUTHOR

Ryuho Okawa, founder and spiritual leader of the Institute for Research in Human Happiness (IRH), has devoted his life to the exploration of the spirit world and ways to human happiness.

He was born in 1956 in Tokushima, Japan. After graduating from the University of Tokyo, he joined a major Tokyo based trading house and studied international finance at the Graduate Center of the City University of New York. In 1986, he renounced his business career and established IRH.

He has been designing IRH spiritual workshops for people from all walks of life, from teenagers to business executives. He is known for his wisdom, compassion and commitment to educating people to think and act in spiritual and religious ways.

The members of IRH follow the path he teaches, ministering to people who need help by spreading his teachings.

He is the author of many books and periodicals, including *The Laws of the Sun*, *The Laws of Eternity*, *The Essence of Buddha*, *The Starting Point of Happiness* and *Love, Nurture and Forgive*. He has also produced successful feature length films (including animations) based on his works.

Want to know more?

Thank you for choosing this book. If you would like to receive further information about titles by Ryuho Okawa, please send the following information either by fax, post or e-mail to your nearest IRH Branch.

1. Title Purchased

_____

2. Please let us know your impression of this book.

_____

3. Are you interested in receiving a catalog of Ryuho Okawa's books?

        Yes ❑   No ❑

4. Are you interested in receiving IRH Monthly?

        Yes ❑   No ❑

Name : Mr / Mrs / Ms / Miss :_____

Address : _____

_____

_____

Phone: _____

Email: _____

Thank you for your interest in Lantern Books.